The
INCREDIBLE
BOOK of
OUTRAGEOUS
FACTS for KIDS

The
INCREDIBLE
BOOK *of*
OUTRAGEOUS
FACTS *for* KIDS
Random Information
YOU NEED TO KNOW!

Nancy Furstinger

Sky Pony Press
New York, NY

*For my brother, Frank, sister-in-law Janelle,
and nephews Doug and Joe, who will especially
appreciate the Wacky Sports section.*
—Nancy Furstinger

Visit our website at www.skyponypress.com.

10 9 8 7 6 5 4 3 2 1

Manufactured in China, April 2024
This product conforms to CPSIA 2008

Library of Congress Cataloging-in-Publication Data is available on file.

Cover design by David Ter-Avanesyan & Erin Seward-Hiatt
Cover photographs: Getty Images
Written by Nancy Furstinger
Edited by Nicole Frail
Interior design by Joshua Barnaby
A special thank-you to John Munley

Print ISBN: 978-1-5107-7122-2
Ebook ISBN: 978-1-5107-7123-9

Contents

The INCREDIBLE BOOK of OUTRAGEOUS FACTS for KIDS

Amazing Animals

Raise your paw, er, hand if you think that animals are awesome. A multitude of amazing animals share our planet, and each year scientists discover more. From the bizarre to the unbelievable, these fascinating animal facts will astonish you . . . and they're all true!

—

Did you know that, just like harried humans, jackals use babysitters? These wild dog moms can hunt knowing that other pack members are protecting the pups.

Satanic leaf-tailed geckos have tiny horns and red eyes.

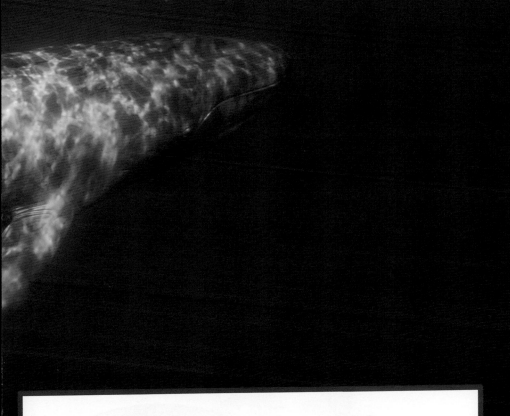

**Blue whales are gigantic!
Here are some fun facts about
the biggest animal on Earth:**

1. Blue whales stretch about the length of three school buses.
2. Their hearts are around the size of a small car, and their tongues weigh as much as an Asian elephant.
3. A human could swim through their enormous blood vessels.
4. Their jumbo-sized babies, called calves, drink fifty gallons of whale milk each day and can gain ten pounds per hour.
5. Blue whales are the loudest animals on Earth. How loud? Louder than a jet!

Chameleons change color to signal different moods, such as red to warn that they're angry.

Think polar bears' fur is white? It's actually made up of clear tubes of hair designed to reflect light and help them blend into their Arctic habitat.

The 150,000 muscles in elephants' trunks help them to knock down trees or pick up a strand of straw.

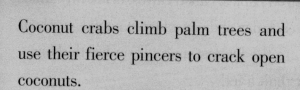

Coconut crabs climb palm trees and use their fierce pincers to crack open coconuts.

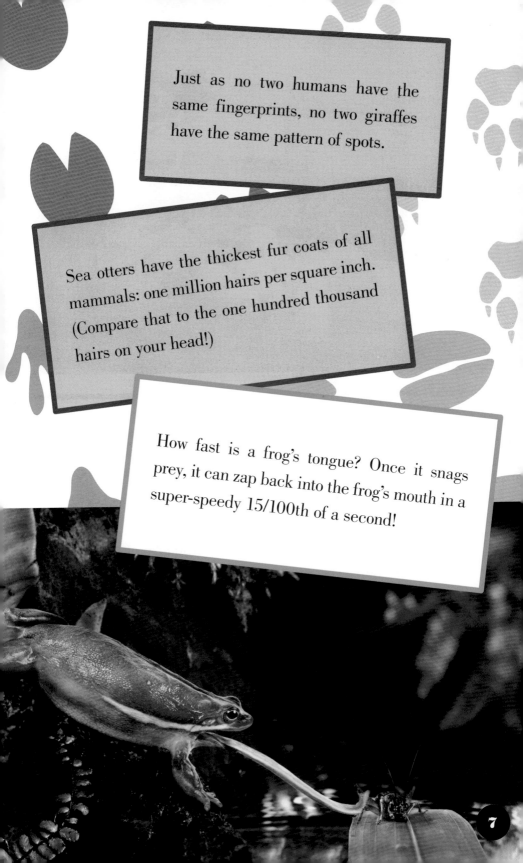

Just as no two humans have the same fingerprints, no two giraffes have the same pattern of spots.

Sea otters have the thickest fur coats of all mammals: one million hairs per square inch. (Compare that to the one hundred thousand hairs on your head!)

How fast is a frog's tongue? Once it snags prey, it can zap back into the frog's mouth in a super-speedy 15/100th of a second!

Everything about the world's largest and heaviest bird is amazing! Did you know these ostrich facts?

1. Ostriches have huge eyes around the size of billiard balls; their eyes are bigger than their brains.
2. Males can measure nine feet tall. Of course, their necks make up half of that.
3. Although these birds can't fly, they can sprint up to forty-five miles per hour.
4. Females lay giant eggs that weigh three pounds—about as heavy as twenty-four chicken eggs!
5. A powerful kick from an ostrich can kill a lion.

Female sea turtles can swim thousands of miles to dig their nests on the same beach where they themselves hatched. Scientists think they use the positions of the moon and the stars along with Earth's magnetic fields to plot their course, like an internal GPS.

The warts on male warthogs protect them during fights by shielding their eyes and jaws from rivals' tusks.

A super sense of smell allows great white sharks to sniff out a single drop of blood floating in ten billion drops of water.

A saw-whet owl hitched a 170-mile ride inside New York City's Rockefeller Center Christmas tree. She made a complete recovery, thanks to fluids and all the mice she could eat, then continued on her journey south.

Turkey vultures have a terrific sense of smell. Natural gas companies use these vultures to find gas leaks. The leaking gas smells just like the dead animal that turkey vultures devour.

Do you think alligators look prehistoric? That's because they're an ancient species whose relatives evolved eighty million years ago—before the first dinosaurs!

Beavers are clever engineers famous for building dams. They change their environment more than any other animal on the planet . . . except for humans.

Bald eagles have such a strong grip that they can seize prey nearly half their body weight, but sometimes huge fish drag them beneath the water.

Newborns munching on their mothers? When legless baby amphibians called caecilians are hatched, they use baby teeth to peel off the outer layer of their mother's skin and gobble it up to gain energy.

Snub-nosed monkeys have upturned noses that cause them to sneeze when raindrops splash in their faces.

You couldn't beat a sailfish in a race: it leaps and swims at blind speeds of up to sixty-nine miles per hour.

An adult pangolin can gobble seventy million insect pests such as termites each year. Not bad for an animal that looks like a cross between an artichoke and a pine cone!

Male southern elephant seals sport inflatable noses that they blow up to look like elephant trunks. They use it to make roaring sounds to attract females.

Giant pandas start out tiny. They weigh about the same size at birth as a stick of butter.

Male humpback whales sing songs of repeating patterns to find mates. Their songs can travel twenty miles through the ocean and last for hours at a time.

Did you know that endangered black rhinos can "fly"? To be transported to a protected habitat, they are sedated and then suspended by their ankles from helicopters.

It can take sloths thirty days to poop out one leaf. No wonder they only take a bathroom break once per week!

The octopus is a remarkable mollusk. Which of these facts surprise you?

1. The blue-ringed octopus can kill a human with a single bite.
2. If an octopus loses a tentacle, it will regrow another one.
3. Using muscles, an octopus can change skin colors with super speed.
4. Blue blood keeps the octopus alive in extreme temperatures.
5. One brainy octopus escaped from an aquarium by pushing out of his tank, traveling down a pipe, and splashing back into the sea!

A dolphin rests half of its brain while it sleeps while the other half stays awake. If it senses danger, both halves spring into action, alerting the dolphin.

African pouched rats use their superior sense of smell to sniff out hidden landmines and detect tuberculosis.

When a thirteen-foot-long Burmese python tried to gobble a six-foot-long American alligator in Everglades National Park, the snake exploded.

Why are penguins able to drink salt water? A pair of glands filters salt from their blood.

Instead of roaring like lions and tigers, cheetahs chirp and yelp.

Adorable amphibians called axolotls have surprising super powers:

1. If they lose one of their arms or legs to a predator, no problem: they can regrow a new one.
2. And they can replace that limb one hundred times!
3. These salamanders can rebuild other body parts such as crushed jaws and spines—and even parts of their brains.
4. Scientists can even transplant body parts from one axolotl to another.
5. Even as adults, axolotls look the same as tadpoles. They have external gills on stalks that make them look as if they're wearing feathered fuchsia crowns.

The blobfish's droopy scowl and blobby body helped it win the title of the world's ugliest animal.

Gray wolves can gobble up to twenty pounds of food in one meal. This gives new meaning to wolfing down one's food!

The bumblebee bat weighs less than a dime and is about as long as a paper clip.

What won't the male bowerbird do to dazzle a female? He'll weave a fancy nest and decorate it with blue objects like bottle caps and flowers. Then he'll perform a crazy dance while buzzing. Impressive!

The Tasmanian devil not only eats carrion (dead flesh!), but it also snoozes inside the rotten carcass.

Orangutans are the largest animals that live in trees. Every night they speed-build new sleeping nests high above the rain forest.

The world's strangest parrot lives on the ground and climbs trees. In fact, at eight pounds, the kakapo is too heavy to fly.

Spadefoot toads grow superfast before their ponds dry up. Their eggs can hatch within a day, and tadpoles undergo metamorphosis in just two weeks.

The next time you call someone a pigeon brain, consider how brilliant these birds are. Pigeons can understand abstract concepts like time and space and can tell a Monet painting from a Picasso.

Imagine living in an underwater cave for one hundred years and eating only once each decade! Impossible, you say? The olm, a blind salamander, has these amazing abilities.

Vampire bats share a mouthful of blood with roost mates whose hunt ended in failure. These bats need to slurp blood every three days or they'll starve.

This animal is full of surprises: it has a beak and webbed feet and lays eggs, but it's not a duck.

1. The platypus is one of only two mammals that lays eggs (the other is the equally bizarre echidna).
2. After the eggs hatch, babies nurse on milk that flows from pores on their mother's skin.
3. Males have hollow spurs on their hind feet that deliver venom to rivals during mating season.
4. Thousands of cells in the platypus bill sense electrical currents generated by live prey.
5. No teeth? No problem—the platypus scoops up gravel from riverbeds to grind up insects, shellfish, and worms.

An ocean clam called a quahog has an incredible life span. Scientists counted the annual growth bands on one clam's shell and discovered that it was 507 years old!

Baby porcupines are born with soft quills that harden in a few days.

The male tufted deer has long upper canines that protrude from his mouth like vampire fangs.

Horned lizards have a wild trick to deter predators: they squirt blood from the corners of their eyes.

The hummingbird is the only bird species that can fly backward.

Male seahorses carry eggs in their brood pouches for two to four weeks and then give birth to up to 1,500 babies.

The wombat marks the entrance of its burrow with square-shaped poop that won't roll away: keep out!

Skunks can shoot a super-stinky spray up to ten feet using a gland underneath their tails.

Barreleye fish have a transparent head with bizarre tubular eyes that glow green.

Naked mole rats have lips that close behind their big buckteeth so they can dig tunnels without sucking dirt into their lungs.

The aye-aye uses its long bony middle fingers to scoop grubs out of trees.

Blue dragons are real-life Pokémon: these sea slugs float upside down in the ocean and use rows of needle-sharp teeth to snag jellyfish. No jellies around? Blue dragons will gobble each other!

The male superb bird of paradise fans his neck cape, snaps his tail feathers, and hops around the female in a wild courtship dance. Talk about getting your groove on!

Not all male peafowl have majestic green and blue tail feathers. Some have a genetic mutation called leucism that turns a peacock's plumage snowy white.

Narwhals have been called "unicorns of the sea." How many facts do you know about this strange creature?

1. Males have a single long tusk, which is actually a protuding tooth.
2. Narwhals use their tusks not only as a hunting tool, but also to establish rank.
3. Tusks have up to ten million nerve endings that help narwhals "see" underwater by touching and tasting.
4. *Narwhal* came from combining two old Norse words meaning "corpse" and "whale" because the animal's mottled color looks like the skin of drowned sailors.
5. These whales can dive down as far as a mile and a half deep!

You now know 86 facts about AMAZING ANIMALS!

Genius Kids

What makes a kid a genius? Read on to find out. Maybe we can add *your* name to this list?

—

Gitanjali Rao is a teenage scientist and inventor who problem-solves and inspires other students.

1. At age eleven, she created a device to test for lead contamination in drinking water.
2. Gitanjali designed *Kindly*—a phone and Web tool that can detect cyberbullying.
3. Using genetics, she's working on products to diagnose opioid addiction and to detect parasites in water.
4. She runs innovation workshops where she's mentored more than thirty thousand students.
5. No wonder Gitanjali became *Time* magazine's first-ever Kid of the Year, in 2020!

How does a rescue organization discover which dogs are kid-friendly? Mt. Rottie Rescue pulls dogs from a shelter in Kentucky and sends them north to foster homes to prepare them for adoption. Enter Amyia, a young dog whisperer who kid-tests foster dogs to determine their friendliness.

Tyler Gordon has faced challenges including a stutter that he was bullied over. Now he speaks out using his artistic voice by painting portraits of Black leaders and helping other kids through his videos on his YouTube channel, Tongue Ty'd.

When William Kamkwamba was fourteen, his Malawi village was hit by a drought. Using library books, he built a windmill out of junkyard scraps that brought electricity to his village.

Elaina Smith got a radio gig offering advice to adult listeners. She was hired after she told a woman who broke up with her boyfriend to "go bowling with pals and drink a mug of milk." The seven-year-old became the youngest broadcaster in Britain.

Another young talk show host, Daniel Cook, began hosting his own preschool TV series at the age of six. Kids tune into *This Is Daniel Cook* to join the host on exciting adventures like digging for dinosaur bones.

Priyanshi Somani set a new world record when she won the Mental Calculation World Cup at age eleven, calculating square roots in her head.

Michael Kearney also set world records. He learned to read at only ten months old; he graduated from college at age ten; and he started teaching college at sixteen.

Another child prodigy, Sergey Karjakin, became the youngest ever chess grand master at age twelve.

Greta Thunberg, the Swedish environmental activist, has millions of supporters around the world.

1. She gained international attention when she skipped school to call attention to climate change.
2. Greta's protest started a movement among students called Fridays for Future.
3. She's given speeches about global warming to powerful leaders.
4. Her activism, known as "the Greta Effect," has motivated young people to take action for the health of our planet.
5. Climate change helped her overcome challenges associated with Asperger's syndrome and speak out, inspiring others with the spectrum disorder.

High school student Michael Sessions was sworn in as the youngest United States mayor at age eighteen, working out of his bedroom office after finishing his homework.

Akrit Jaswal performed surgery in a remote village in India to separate the fused fingers of a burn victim. Although he wasn't a doctor, the seven-year-old had a reputation as a medical genius.

Victor De Leon III, who goes by the name of Lil Poison, became the world's youngest professional video gamer when Major League Gaming signed him up at the age of six.

Amanda Gorman zoomed into fame at President Joe Biden's inauguration. Now her words are being read around the world.

1. Before she stepped on the national stage, Amanda was chosen as the Youth Poet Laureate of Los Angeles when she was sixteen.
2. When she read her poem "The Hill We Climb," Amanda became the youngest poet to recite at a presidential inauguration.
3. Amanda struggles with a speech impediment (as does President Biden), but she practiced and delivered a flawless reading.
4. She's written a children's book, *Change Sings,* as a call to action for kids to make changes.
5. Her nonprofit—One Pen One Page—empowers young people to use their voices and pens to help eliminate inequality through education.

An eight-year-old girl created her own brand of crayons: More Than Peach. Bellen Woodard wanted kids to have multicultural crayons to match all their skin tones.

Mikhail Ali officially became recognized as a genius when he joined Mensa, a group open to people with IQs in the top 2 percent of the population. The supersmart three-year-old is nicknamed the Human Calculator for his math skills.

Another talented three-year-old took voice and piano lessons. Five years later, Gwyn Mackenzie wowed audiences by singing arias in four languages.

Two-year-old Guyland Leday taught himself to play the accordion zydeco-style. After six years of practicing, he was featured in a documentary *The Music in Me.*

Mensa member Mike Wimmer graduated from high school and earned his associate's degree all in the same year. Plus the twelve-year-old is busy running two start-up companies that aim to help make people's lives easier through advanced technologies and robotics.

Jordan Reeves was born without the bottom half of her left arm, but she didn't let her limb difference hold her back. The tween put her STEM skills to work designing 3-D printable prosthetics that shoot glitter and hosting design workshops through her nonprofit Born Just Right.

A class of fourth-grade students in Texas started and ran their own animal shelter. DAWGS has rescued and rehomed more than twenty thousand animals thanks to kids who believed they could make a difference.

Ian McKenna has been gardening since he was four, and he put his green thumb to work in third grade when he planted a school garden to feed low-income families. McKenna's Giving Gardens have expanded to other schools and provided ten tons of organic produce.

When seven-year-old Nancy Yi Fan and her family moved to the United States, she taught herself English by reading books. After mastering a new language, she wrote *Snowbird*, a fantasy novel that launched her to the top of the *New York Times* bestseller list at the age of thirteen.

How many three-year-olds know the names of all fifty US state capitals, plus the capitals of more than a hundred countries? At that young age, Adrian Aivaliotis could reel them off.

Another geography genius, Lilly Gaskin, could point out seventy-eight different countries on a map when she was just two years old.

Kishan Shrikanth dreams of becoming the next Steven Spielberg. At the age of ten, this Bollywood director already made his mark on the big screen, becoming the youngest filmmaker of a feature film.

A young boy used his imagination and his summer vacation to build a cardboard arcade in his father's auto parts store. Thanks to a short video that went viral, nine-year-old Caine Monroy and his arcade have raised more than $242,000 for his scholarship fund.

If there was a kids' version of *Dancing with the Stars*, two seven-year-old ballroom dancers could judge the show. Rickie Taylor and Erik Linder won a top prize in the USA Dance National Championships, where they danced the foxtrot, jive, and waltz.

Piano prodigy Ethan Bortnick began composing at the age of five. He has a musical memory that allows him to listen to a song once and then play it. As the world's youngest solo musician to headline his own concert tour, Ethan has performed around the globe while helping raise more than $50,000,000 for charities.

Fraser Doherty learned jam-making in his grandmother's kitchen in Scotland. At fourteen, the teen turned his passion into SuperJam and became one of the youngest suppliers to a major supermarket.

An Australian abstract artist began painting at nine months old. Aelita Andre had her first solo exhibition at the age of two.

Kim Ung Yong understood algebra at eight months old, and by the time this Korean supergenius was four, he could fluently speak English, German, Japanese, and Korean.

Another young entrepreneur combined her love of challenges and problem-solving. Noa Mintz started Nannies by Noa to pair clients with skilled childcare workers. Her business became so successful that she hired a CEO so she could focus on schoolwork.

After getting stung by bees, Mikaila Ulmer turned her fear into forgiveness by launching Me & the Bees Lemonade. Sales of the teen's honey-sweetened drink skyrocketed, and she donates some of her profits to help save honeybees.

Moziah Bridges became a CEO of Mo's Bows when he was a teenager. The young fashion designer creates eye-catching bow ties and neckties, including for all thirty National Basketball Association teams.

Shubham Banerjee invented Braigo, a low-cost braille printer, when he was only twelve. His portable machine allows people to print out braille—the tactile writing system for people who have visual impairments.

Who doesn't dream about getting rich by creating an app? Nick D'Aloisio invented Summly, an application that condenses news articles into 350–400 words for busy readers. The teenage entrepreneur struck it rich when Yahoo paid $30 million for his app!

Frustrated by being overlooked while on vacation, twelve-year-old Bella Tipping launched an online travel review site designed for kids. Now families can use Kidzcationz.com to make sure vacations will be fun for everyone.

Mason Andrews set a world record when, at eighteen, he became the youngest person to fly solo around the world. His circumnavigation took seventy-six days.

Nihar Janga has set two world records. At age eleven, he became the youngest winner of the Scripps National Spelling Bee. (His final word was *gesellschaft*.) Three years later, he triumphed at the National Geographic Bee, becoming the first person to win both competitions.

Malala Yousafzai is known around the world for her activism and for inspiring other girls to take action.

1. At the age of eleven, Malala began blogging anonymously for the British Broadcasting Corporation. She spoke out about life in Pakistan under the Taliban, who threatened to deny girls an education.
2. Malala gained global attention when the Taliban shot her in the head. Then just fifteen years old, she recovered after multiple surgeries and continued to advocate for education.
3. At the age of seventeen, the teen became the youngest person to win the Nobel Peace Prize.
4. Malala enjoys watching cartoons as an escape from reality.
5. In 2015, an asteroid was named in honor of the teenager. Asteroid 316201 Malala is located in the main asteroid belt between Mars and Jupiter.

When fourteen-year-old Nathan Lu uploaded aerial images he took to a digital mapping service, he scored the world record for becoming the youngest drone cartographer.

Amber Kelley is inspiring other kids to have fun in the kitchen. After the teen won *Food Network Star Kids*, she hosted her own web series on the network and wrote a cookbook.

While practicing lacrosse, Rachel Zietz became exasperated when the equipment fell apart. This spurred the teen to launch Gladiator Lacrosse, which offers durable yet affordable equipment and has generated $7 million in revenue.

Mihir Garimella has won awards for solving problems using tech solutions, such as a robot that tunes violins after listening to sound samples. The teen specializes in designing drones, like one that can be used in search and rescue to find people trapped after earthquakes.

Boyan Slat started The Ocean Cleanup to rid the world's oceans of plastic. His system uses wide floating pipes with a screen beneath them to trap plastic in the Great Pacific Garbage Patch and other polluted spots.

Nine-year-old Milo Cress founded Be Straw Free when he noticed drinks came with plastic straws, which are not accepted at recycling facilities. His project aims to reduce unnecessary plastic waste, such as the 390 million straws Americans use every day.

Buddy Benches are springing up on playgrounds, offering shy kids a place to make new friendships. Sammie Vance decided to collect more than sixteen hundred pounds of plastic bottle caps and have them recycled into benches.

When Andini Makosinski heard that a friend in the Philippines couldn't study at night due to a lack of electricity, the teen invented the Hollow Flashlight that runs off the heat of your hand. No batteries required!

An inventor since age four, Xóchitl Guadalupe Cruz López invented a rooftop solar water heater using recycled stuff, such as hoses, glass panels, and plastic bottles. Her environmentally friendly heater won a science prize from the National Autonomous University of Mexico.

Benjamin Firester won a top young science award for his computer model that can predict potato late blight, which causes billions of dollars in lost crops every year.

Another teenage scientist won first place in an international fair for his new system to improve spinal surgery. Inspiration struck while Krithik Ramesh was playing a video game: he used the same motion-tracking technology to develop his safer and more accurate navigation system.

While working in their high school lab, Miranda Wang and Jeanny Yao discovered soil-based bacteria capable of eating plastic. Their start-up, BioCellection, aims to break down previously nonrecyclable trash, such as plastic bags, transforming each ton into $2,500 worth of valuable chemicals.

Faithe Herman, who played Annie on the TV show *This Is Us*, speaks out about dissection in the classroom. The actor urges students to request humane alternatives, such as virtual dissection.

Teenager Dasia Taylor juiced beets and used this natural dye for her invention: a "smart" suture thread that changes color when a surgical wound becomes infected.

You now know 71 facts about GENIUS KIDS!

Wacky Sports

Calling all sports fans: Which of these games would you like to play or watch?

—

The World Alternative Games are held in the United Kingdom. Laughter is the buzzword for spectators watching zany sports such as:

1. **Man vs. Horse Marathon:** runners and cyclists compete against horseback riders along a challenging and muddy twenty-two-mile course.

2. **Worm Charming:** contestants stake out patches of ground and compete to see how many worms they can bring to the surface.

3. **Bathtubbing:** people race each other or against a stopwatch in bathtubs propelled by motors or paddled like canoes.

4. **Underwater Hockey:** teams push a heavy puck along the bottom of a swimming pool while wearing snorkels.

5. **Pooh Sticks:** named in honor of Winnie the Pooh, this simple sport involves standing on a bridge and dropping sticks into the water, then racing to the other side to see whose stick is the winner.

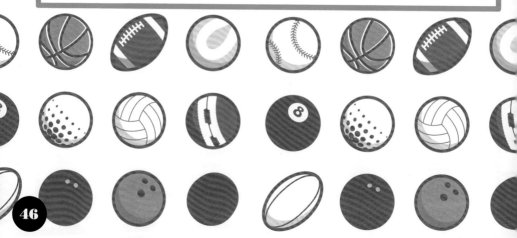

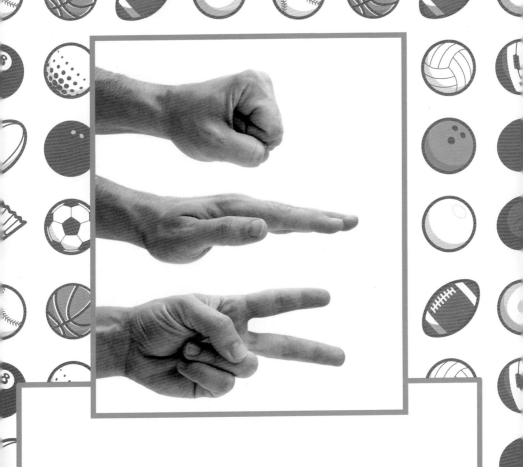

6. Rock, Paper, Scissors: this playground hand game between two players is more about strategy than luck, with the most skilled players reacting in split seconds.

7. Bog Snorkeling: contestants don snorkels and flippers to race two sixty-yard lengths in a marshy trench; wet suits are optional.

8. Cheese Rolling: people race a seven-pound hunk of cheese down a steep hill at speeds of up to thirty miles per hour.

In rabbit agility competitions, pet rabbits hop over, under, around, and through equipment in a ring. Races are timed and the speediest rabbit wins the contest.

You've probably heard of horse polo, but how about bicycle polo? Teams riding bikes use mallets to hit a small ball into their opponent's goal.

For the Wife Carrying Championship, male competitors race through a special obstacle course while carrying a female teammate.

Not to be outdone, there's a husband dragging race, in which women pull their partners down a slippery slope. At the bottom, the males perform chores, such as changing diapers.

In a tomahawk throwing competition, participants aim their axes at targets similar to those used in archery. Don't forget the first aid kit!

Or perhaps you'd like to try your hand at caber tossing, a contest of strength where competitors hurl a long heavy log so it flips over straight.

How about a few less dangerous sports? Speedcubing involves twisting pieces of combination puzzles such as Rubik's Cube as fast as possible. Challenges include playing with one hand or blindfolded.

Sport stacking also requires speed and dexterity to stack nine or twelve cups in special formations.

The National Marbles Tournament hosts more than twelve hundred games over four days. . . .

Two champions and two sportsmanship winners receive college scholarships: something worth shooting for!

Here's a fun contest designed just for kids (and those who are young at heart): the World Puddle Jumping Championships. Top scores go to the highest jumpers, the most enthusiastic players, and the competitors who end up with the most mud sticking to them!

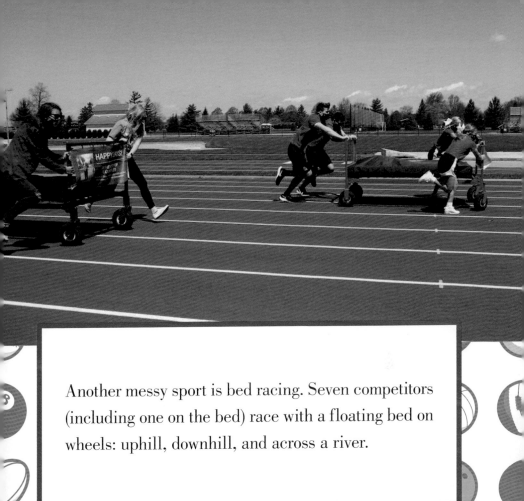

Another messy sport is bed racing. Seven competitors (including one on the bed) race with a floating bed on wheels: uphill, downhill, and across a river.

Babies can strut their stuff in the Baby Games, Olympics-inspired events for kids five years old and under. Sports stars of the future can run or crawl, kick and throw balls, and lift weights.

Animals are fun to watch, especially if they're racing. Check out these crazy animal competitions:

1. The Jumping Frog Jubilee is inspired by a tall tale written by Mark Twain. Frogs compete to break the world record of 21 feet, 5¾ inches set by Rosie the Ribeter in 1986.
2. In the Scotland Island 500, canine contestants paddle across a stretch of water.
3. Hamsters race down a course in balls fitted to miniature racing cars. The record to beat for crossing the finish line is thirty-eight seconds.

4. Trained pigs race around a small track, up a ramp, and jump into a pool—proving that pigs really can fly, at least for a few seconds.

5. Perhaps the slowest sport in the world, snail races start in the middle of a circular track. The first snail to touch the border of the circle wins.

6. In a slightly faster race, families line up on beaches to cheer on hermit crabs to victory.

7. And finally there's cockroach racing, which is self-explanatory!

One of the wildest races takes place in Colorado. In the World Championship Pack Burro Race, a team of human runners and burros race either fifteen or thirty miles. According to the rules, "the runner may push, pull, drag, or carry the burro," but they must cross the finish line together.

What do you get when you combine volleyball, soccer, and extreme gymnastics? It's Bossaball—a wild new sport played on an inflatable court with trampolines while music pulsates!

Another combo sport, FootGolf, is a mash up of soccer and golf. Players kick soccer balls into holes on courses—the lowest number of kicks wins.

Disc Golf blends Frisbee with golf. Players throw a flying disc at targets such as elevated metal baskets. Again, the fewest throws wins.

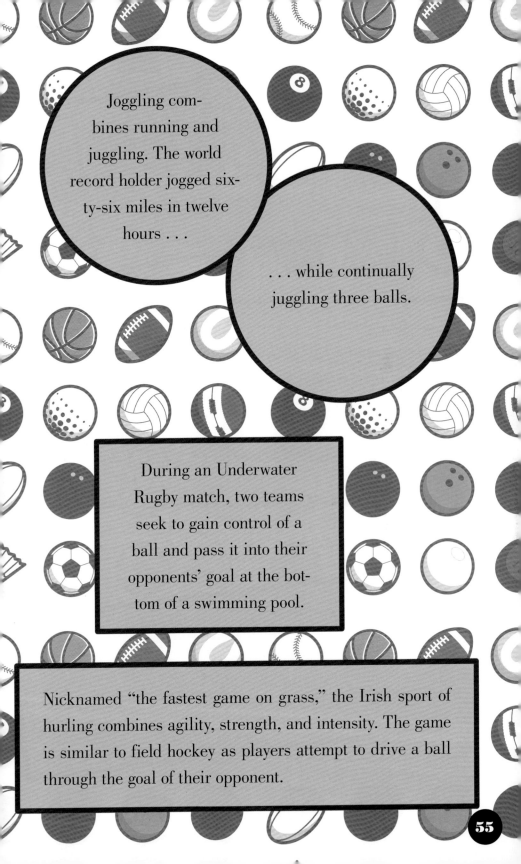

Joggling combines running and juggling. The world record holder jogged sixty-six miles in twelve hours . . .

. . . while continually juggling three balls.

During an Underwater Rugby match, two teams seek to gain control of a ball and pass it into their opponents' goal at the bottom of a swimming pool.

Nicknamed "the fastest game on grass," the Irish sport of hurling combines agility, strength, and intensity. The game is similar to field hockey as players attempt to drive a ball through the goal of their opponent.

Imagine playing hockey while balancing on a single wheel. That's unicycle hockey—an offbeat version of the sport that's sometimes even played with the puck set on fire!

Maybe you read about Quidditch—the sport played by witches and wizards riding flying broomsticks—in the Harry Potter book series. There's also a real-life version that mixes dodgeball, rugby, and tag while teammates play with brooms between their legs.

How about a sport where people fly? Birdman rallies around the world feature different events ranging from homemade flying machines to hang gliders flown by experienced pilots. Fliers leap from jetties or bridges and compete for distance.

Exciting collisions and crashes are part of roller derby! Two teams consisting of one jammer and four blockers roller-skate around an oval ring; jammers attempt to skate by their opponent's blockers.

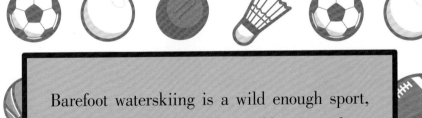

Barefoot waterskiing is a wild enough sport, but combine it with being towed by an airplane and it becomes super thrilling.

It's fun and games for dogs when they enter canine competitions such as these:

1. Frisbee canine competitions got their start when Ashley Whippet thrilled crowds with his nine-foot leaps in the air to catch discs. Now dogs of every size fetch flying disks in aerial acrobatics.

2. In Flyball relay races, each dog on a team jumps over hurdles, bounces its paws on a box that shoots a tennis ball into the air, catches the ball, and returns to the starting line. The fastest team wins.

3. People race alongside their dogs as they run through agility obstacle courses that include weave poles, A-frames, tire jumps, seesaws, and tunnels.

4. Herding breeds such as border collies compete in sheepdog trials where they guide livestock—cattle, sheep, goats, or ducks—through courses.

5. And instead of livestock, dogs herd flocks of huge exercise balls in the German sport of Treibball.

6. In the wet and wild sport of Diving Dogs, a handler tosses a ball and the dog dashes along a dock, leaps into the pool, and retrieves the ball. The dog with the longest jump wins.

7. You've heard of ballroom dancing; now there's canine freestyle dancing! Dogs and their handlers move to the music in routines that include pivoting, spinning, jumping, and bowing.

8. Dogs performing hang ten maneuvers? In dog surfing competitions, water-loving dogs of all sizes catch waves on surfboards and are judged by the size of the wave and how long they stay on the boards.

9. Skijoring combines cross-country skiing and dogsledding. In this winter sport, one to three dogs help pull a skier through the snow.

Kite fighting is popular in Asian countries. Fighter kites fly in battles where the goal is to cut opponents' lines using ground glass glued onto kite strings.

Pogo sticks were trendy toys in the 1920s. Today, thrill seekers use extreme pogo sticks that bounce so high they can leap over small buildings in one bound.

Stunt cyclists also need incredible balance. One performed a neat feat when he zoomed down a steep hill backward while doing a wheelie.

Whitewater rapids, gigantic waves and rocks, waterfalls—no wonder rafting races can be rigorous and risky. Competitors need exceptional rafting skills to master these challenging river courses.

Adrenaline junkies like cliff divers thrive on danger. These highly trained athletes make death-defying dives from heights of up to 148 feet above the water.

Paintball is a more extreme version of the children's game of hide-and-seek and tag. Players eliminate opponents by tagging them with paintballs fired out of mechanical guns.

Maybe you've watched your hamster racing around inside an exercise ball and thought it looked like fun. Well, let the good times roll: zorbing allows humans to roll downhill inside huge inflatable orbs. Here are the two world records to beat: fastest speed at thirty-two miles per hour and longest distance of 1,870 feet.

There's surfboarding, sandboarding, and now volcano surfing. Riders stand, sit, or lie down on boards while surfing on either active or inactive volcanoes.

In the wild sailing sport of kitesurfing, surfers harness the power of the wind with a large kite that propels them across the water.

Hot air balloons cannot fly beyond the atmosphere, but pilot Vijaypat Singhania set a world record for the highest flight when his specially designed balloon reached an altitude of 69,850 feet.

One of the most bizarre sports is extreme ironing, where people compete to iron clothes in the strangest spots, like underwater and above the Mount Everest Base Camp!

Superhuman triathletes tackle the Ironman World Championship, a grueling 140.6-mile race that combines swimming, biking, and running. And yes, despite the name, there's a women's division.

You'll need a huge appetite along with a strong stomach to excel in competitive eating sports. Ready, set, open your mouth, and *go*!

1. Who doesn't love Halloween candy? Your dentist would schedule time with you in the chair if you won the candy-bowl contest. Winner Matt Stonie gobbled 65.9 ounces of the sweet stuff (that's more than four pounds) in six minutes!

2. Professional speed eaters enter the Nathan's Famous International Hot Dog Eating Contest on the Fourth of July in Coney Island. But can they beat the twelve-time champ, Joey Chestnut, who downed seventy-four hot dogs and buns in ten minutes?

3. Yum, cheesecake! You might never look at a slice the same way again after inhaling eleven pounds in nine minutes like Sonya Thomas!

4. Fearsome competitor Juliet Lee won the Ultimate Eating Tournament: seven chicken wings, one pound of nachos, three hot dogs, two personal pizzas, and three Italian ices in seven minutes, thirteen seconds.

5. Jim Reeves was ready to bust a gut after gorging on 13.22 pounds of watermelon in fifteen minutes. Wonder if he had time to spit out the seeds?

6. Michelle Lesco smashed a previous record when she slurped up a bowl of pasta in 26.69 seconds.

7. Some people chow down on strange things. Richard LeFevre set world records eating six pounds of Spam from the can in twelve minutes and 247 pickled peppers in eight minutes.

8. You won't want to sit downwind of Gideon Oji after he won a challenge eating ten pounds of baked beans in one minute, forty-five seconds!

9. Imagine eating 61.75 ears of sweet corn in twelve minutes flat. Carmen Cincotti earned this record . . .guess he couldn't finish that final ear!

10. George Chiger gulped down two eight-ounce cans of spray cheese in fifty-nine seconds. Does this even qualify as food?

11. Pie-eating contests are always a blast to watch, especially if there's a no-hands-allowed rule. Patrick Bertoletti holds the record for consuming 9.17 pounds of blueberry pie hands-free in eight minutes.

12. Cookie Jarvis devoured one gallon, nine ounces of vanilla ice cream in twelve minutes. Talk about brain freeze!

You now know 72 facts about WACKY SPORTS!

Offbeat Foods

People around the world can have strange tastes in food. Different dishes are fun to read about, and maybe even sample; others are stomach churning. Which of these would you chomp down on or slurp up?

—

**Some foods are deliciously dangerous
and can even be deadly.
Eat these at your own risk!**

1. The names of these mushrooms should offer a clue:
   death cap and destroying angel. Eat them and you
   might need a liver transplant to survive.
2. There's enough poison in one pufferfish to kill thirty
   people, with a deadly dose smaller than a pinhead!
   But that doesn't stop specially trained chefs in Japan
   from preparing this fish, using a special knife to cut
   out the poison parts. One bad cut could turn this into
   a last supper for the diner.

3. Who doesn't love strawberry rhubarb pie? But don't accidentally bake the rhubarb leaves, which contain an acid that could kill you.

4. Aside from being a processed meat product, the humble hot dog is the top choking hazard in children under the age of three.

5. Casu marzu is an Italian sheep's milk cheese writhing with maggots. Not only are the maggots alive, but they can also jump up to six inches in the air!

6. Raw octopus is popular in sushi restaurants, but some diners in Korea eat this dish while it's still alive! Then suckers on the wriggling tentacles can stick to the throat and cause suffocation.

7. Don't forget to spit the pits out of those juicy cherries. They contain cyanide, and if you crunch too many pits, they could kill you.

8. Are you allergic to poison ivy? Then you won't want to eat wild cashews. These seeds contain urushiol, the same chemical found in poison ivy, which can kill you if you eat too many. But once they're roasted and shelled, cashews are safe to eat.

Bugs for breakfast, lunch, and dinner? More than two thousand species are consumed around the world, especially in countries where meat is scarce.

1. People in Cambodia snack on deep-fried tarantulas, which are rich in protein. After they're fried in oil, the crispy spiders are seasoned with salt and garlic. Other spots in Southeast Asia sell barbecued tarantulas on a stick.

2. In the deserts of the Australian Outback, Aborigines gather the larvae of ghost moths. They either serve these witchetty grubs fresh off the barbecue or live and raw.

3. Grasshoppers are toasted on griddles, flavored with chili and lime, and sprinkled on guacamole. This crunchy topping is popular in Mexico.

4. Dragonflies are snared with reeds coated in sticky sap. Then they're stir-fried and served over rice in Indonesia.

5. Chefs in New Orleans, Louisiana, also fry dragonflies in vegetable oil and dish them up over sautéed portobello mushrooms.

6. Spicy Critter Fritters are small cakes of fried batters, but the main ingredient is crickets ground into flour. Cricket flour also stars in baked goods like sweet potato brownies.

7. Street food carts in San Francisco, California, serve Mexican cuisine like tortillas stuffed with yellow mealworms and larvae-filled tacos. And for dessert: vanilla ice cream topped with caramelized mealworms.

8. Birds and frogs gobble freaky-looking bugs called cicadas as if they were at an all-you-can-eat buffet. And some people in the United States gorge on dry roasted cicadas sprinkled with salt.

9. Would you try marinated stink bugs? These foul-smelling insects are boiled, then simmered in a Cajun sauce, and dehydrated to a crispy crunch.

10. Pop-ups across Los Angeles serve ant larvae in quiches and blinis (Russian pancakes) and atop corn tortillas.

11. Oven-toasted mealworms are fatty with a nutty flavor, which makes them the perfect replacement for pecans in pecan pie.

12. At first glance, Japanese wasp crackers look like chocolate chip cookies. But those aren't chips—they're digger wasps. Thankfully their powerful stingers no longer work.

13. South Korean markets sell a popular snack: beondegi, crunchy silkworm pupae that's boiled or steamed.

14. In Thailand, tiny scorpions preserved in alcohol are used as garnishes for food and drinks.

15. Still not convinced that bugs belong on the menu? According to the United Nations, edible insects might be the food of the future: they're good for the planet and for people. For example, crickets consume less water than any other protein, and they produce zero greenhouse gases. Plus they contain more protein than beef, more calcium than milk, and more iron than spinach.

Some of the world's strangest foods might cause you to lose your appetite. Which one is your number one nightmare?

1. A tribe in India celebrates a festival with a stew called bule-bulak oying made with boiled rats—including what's considered the tastiest parts: the tails and legs.

2. Have you heard of the Scottish dish called haggis? The minced heart, liver, and lungs of a sheep are mixed with other ingredients and then packed into the animal's stomach and boiled for several hours.

3. Rocky Mountain oysters are not the bivalves of the sea. Instead, they're deep-fried testicles from bulls, bison, pigs, and sheep. That's nuts!

4. Stinkhead is an apt description of this traditional Alaskan dish. Fish heads are buried in the ground until they're fermented.

5. Hákarl is a superstinky Icelandic food. A beheaded shark is buried for several months until it reeks of ammonia.

6. Maybe you eat hard-boiled eggs for breakfast, but people in the Philippines eat balut. These fertilized duck embryos are boiled in the shell.

7. In China, "century" eggs are preserved for a few months, not 100 years. However, this is long enough to turn the egg whites brown and yolks a dark green.

8. Black Ivory coffee is prized as the world's rarest and most expensive. Thai elephants eat coffee cherries and in twelve to seventy-two hours poop them out. Then the cherries are plucked, washed, and roasted.

9. What do you get when you drop a live snake into rice wine and let it steep for several months? Snake wine, served in Asia, is safe to drink because the ethanol in the wine destroys the snake's venom.

10. Bird's nest soup is made from nests built by swiftlets. These Southeast Asian birds construct nests using strands of rubbery saliva. Nests are gathered from the tops of caves, soaked in water, and steamed.

11. Duck blood soup is dished up in Poland, with potato dumplings added to the broth.

12. Durian is called the king of fruits in Southeast Asia. You'll need a machete to whack open the giant spiked shell. The jelly-like fruit inside is creamy and smells noxious, like raw sewage.

13. Black pudding isn't a dessert. Instead it's a mixture of pig's blood, animal fat, and onions squeezed into a sausage casing and eaten in England.

14. Jellied moose nose is a Canadian delicacy; the nose and jowls are boiled in chicken broth and then chilled.

15. Cooked tuna eyes are the size of tennis balls. Japanese chefs braise or sauté the eyeballs so diners can suck them out of the hard exteriors.

16. Vegemite is the yeasty by-product found at the bottom of a barrel after brewing beer. Australians spread this sticky, salty paste on toast.

17. Frogs' legs is a French dish prepared with butter, garlic, and parsley sauce.

18. In the Southwestern United States, southern fried rattlesnake is said to taste similar to frogs' legs.

19. Uni is the Japanese name for the edible part of the sea urchin. The spiny sea creatures look like pincushions. Their bright flesh is served raw or in noodle dishes.

20. Now you can sample some of these foods at Disgusting Food Museums that have sprung up around the world. Which one will you try first?

Canned food has certainly come a long way since the early 1800s, when it first burst onto the scene with bland offerings such as beef and peas. Today, if you need to whip up a speedy meal, you're certain to find something more adventurous than that tin of mystery meat.

1. Bored with canned corn beef? You can always pick up a can of pork brains with milk gravy. The serving suggestion on the front of the can shows the contents stirred into scrambled eggs.
2. For the adventurous, there's smoked rattlesnake in a can. Tastes just like chicken, so the manufacturer claims.
3. Or you might prefer another exotic meat in a can: alligator in Cajun gravy.
4. Different regions have different delicacies. You can find "canned armadillo on the half shell" or "creamed possum with sweet potatoes garnished in coon fat gravy."
5. In a category all by itself is canned "buzzard gizzards marinated in cream sauce."
6. In Finland you can shop for karhu pâté: a mix of bear and pork meat.

7. Swedish reindeer, brandy, and spices are the ingredients in a canned pâté, sold around Christmas. Oh, the irony!

8. Canned Russian herring contains fish mouths with sharp teeth still attached.

9. What could be easier to slap together than a peanut butter and jelly sandwich? How about a canned sandwich with a choice of grape jelly or strawberry jam?

10. Another simple lunch that comes in a can is alphabet-shaped pasta in a cheesy tomato sauce. Go ahead and play with your food!

11. If you don't have time to grab a fast-food cheeseburger, you can get a canned version. Sorry, no fries.

12. Have a craving for BLTs on a camping trip? Pop open a can of bacon, which contains fifty precooked slices.

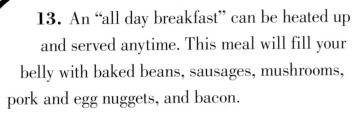

13. An "all day breakfast" can be heated up and served anytime. This meal will fill your belly with baked beans, sausages, mushrooms, pork and egg nuggets, and bacon.

14. Unexpected company for Thanksgiving? Have no fear, there's a fully cooked canned whole chicken, minus the giblets.

15. As a side dish, pop open a can of seven mixed vegetables. These tiny cubes are tricky to eat so they're sometimes encased in aspic, a fancy name for meat jelly.

16. And how about an appetizer? Vienna sausages are made of pork and beef encased in sheep intestines.

17. Or you might prefer tamales from a tin. Filled with chili beef, they're ready to be popped into the microwave.

18. No need for side dishes, appetizers, or dessert when you serve Christmas Tinner. This three-course meal in a tin is made up of nine layers. There's also a twelve-layer vegetarian version and an eleven-layer vegan version.

19. You probably have canned anchovies, sardines, or tuna in your pantry, but your taste buds should wake up with squid in "natural ink."

20. Boiled peanuts have a supershort shelf life so it makes sense to can this Southern snack food.

21. Some street vendors use canned duck fat for deep-frying french fries.

22. Grass jelly can be used as a topping for bubble milk tea. And yes, you can buy this cubed black gelatin in cans.

23. How about an unusual dessert? Chocolate-covered silkworms should hit the spot.

24. Spotted dick sponge pudding is studded with raisins and smothered in custard. But no snickering at the name!

25. If that doesn't tickle your tongue, you can always resort to canned standbys that your grandparents probably ate as children: peaches in heavy syrup, or rice pudding.

Back in the 1950s, the fresh produce sold in markets was humdrum: apples and bananas, potatoes and tomatoes. Then Frieda Rapoport Caplan burst on the scene and changed America's eating habits.

1. Fresh mushrooms were considered exotic when Frieda started working at a huge produce market in Los Angeles, California. She convinced so many customers to try this vegetable that she became known as the Mushroom Queen.

2. She popularized an exotic fruit from New Zealand: Chinese gooseberries. Frieda renamed the fuzzy brown fruit "kiwi" and slowly it became popular.

3. Nothing was too far-out for Frieda. She created fruit and vegetable trends including doughnut peaches, blood oranges, sugar snap peas, and alfalfa sprouts.

4. Frieda transformed American cuisine by introducing more than two hundred exotic fruits and vegetables to supermarkets. That earned her a new nickname: the Mick Jagger of the produce world.

5. When *Star Trek* needed "alien" fruits for an episode, Frieda supplied horned melons: bright orange and spiky with green jelly-like innards.

6. Despite giving out recipes, Frieda never learned to cook.

You now know 74 facts about
OFFBEAT FOODS!

Intriguing Insects and Surprising Spiders

Did you know that there are more than one million species of insects and spiders, with new types awaiting discovery? Some are pests while others are beneficial. These tiny (usually) but mighty creepy-crawlies make up the largest animal species on Earth!

—

Some insects are social. No, they don't have Instagram accounts, but they work together to find food, build nests, and raise their young. Power in numbers!

1. The queen of a termite colony can lay thirty-six thousand eggs each day. And with her lifespan of up to seventy years, that adds up to a mind-boggling number of eggs!

2. Worker termites can build gigantic mounds towering thirty feet tall. Some of these mounds can be spotted from space!

3. Termite soldiers act as if they're at a heavy metal concert when danger invades the nest. Soldiers bang their heads against the walls to send warning vibrations throughout the colony.

4. All the termites in the world combined weigh more than all the humans.

5. Scientists discovered a termite that had been trapped in amber for 100 million years.

6. A colony of thousands of yellow jackets will defend their underground nest. If they feel threatened, they'll swarm out and give chase.

7. Each yellow jacket can sting multiple times. Unlike bees, they have smaller barbs on their stingers that easily pull out.

8. The venom in yellow jackets' stingers can be deadly, causing some people with severe allergies to go into anaphylactic shock.

9. After stinging, yellow jackets will release chemicals that mark you as the enemy. Run away quickly before the angry swarm attacks.

10. Only female yellow jackets sting. They're extremely protective of their nests.

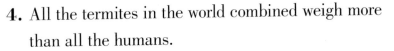

11. Ants have Herculean strength. They can carry objects that weigh fifty times their own body weight. Imagine if you could do that!

12. Some soldier ants use their heads like a cork to block the nest entrance. Worker ants need a special password to return—they touch the guard's head to let this worker know they're part of the colony.

13. When hundreds of thousands of fire ants swarm together, they latch onto each other to form bridges, ladders, and even floating rafts.

14. Fire ants bite, but bullet ants have one of the most painful stings in the world. One scientist described it "like walking over a flaming charcoal with a three-inch nail embedded in your heel."

15. The largest ant's nest was part of a supercolony in Argentina—it stretched more than 3,700 miles wide!

16. Honeybee scouts perform a series of movements called the waggle dance. This teaches other workers the distance and direction where the best food sources can be found.

17. After honeybees load up with pollen and return home to the hive, their wings flap up to fifteen thousand times per minute.

18. If the hive loses its queen bee, workers can create an emergency queen by feeding larvae royal jelly.

19. Honeybees are neat freaks: worker bees remove any dead comrades from the hive and clean up after the queen, the only bee that poops inside.

20. Africanized honeybees escaped from experimental beehives in Brazil. These "killer bees"can chase people more than a quarter mile and attack in huge numbers.

21. Don't even think of hiding in a stream or pond. The killer bee swarm will be waiting when you emerge.

22. As if killer bees aren't scary enough, murder hornets are invading North America. These Asian giant hornets pack a powerful sting, equal to ten yellow jackets stinging at once.

23. The world's largest hornet is gigantic and nasty-looking. They grow up to two inches long with quarter-inch stingers that can pierce beekeeping suits.

24. Murder hornets earned their nickname from preying on honeybees. A raiding party can massacre an entire hive in hours. First they decapitate all the adult bees.

25. Then murder hornets flee with the honeybee larvae. This protein is used to feed the hornets' own brood.

26. Asian giant hornets tagged with radio transmitters are helping scientists to locate nests in search and destroy missions. Before these "Judas" hornets fly back to the nest, they're refueled with strawberry jam.

**Spiders are awesome arachnids!
Their eight legs end in claws, like their
creepy-crawly cousins: scorpions.
Read on for more freaky facts about the
more than 46,700 species of spiders.**

1. Wolf spiders use eight eyes to chase prey. Two huge eyes face forward, two medium face upward, and four tiny eyes line up in a row below. The spiders run, climb, and swim to hunt down insects.

2. The most dangerous spider in North America is the female black widow. The red hourglass on her belly warns: poison. This spider's venom is fifteen times more toxic than a rattlesnake's.

3. How did black widows earn their name? Females sometimes kill the much smaller males after mating. These man-killers seize males with their fangs and then cannibalize them.

4. A male peacock spider uses special dance moves to attract a mate. He'll shake a pair of legs around or raise a flap over his belly and wave it in a fan dance. But if the female becomes bored, she'll gobble up her suitor.

5. Some male peacock spiders have wild patterns and colors. With its black body and white stripes, Skeletorus looks as if it's wearing a skeleton costume. Sparklemuffin has a blue belly with flashy red stripes.

And Nemo has an orange face striped with white, just like the famous clownfish.

6. The Hawaiian happy-face spider sports a smiley face on its belly. This design confuses birds into thinking that the spiders aren't something to eat.

7. Crab spiders use camouflage to confuse enemies. Some spiders change colors to match the different flowers where they hide.

8. Bird dung spiders not only look like piles of bird droppings, but they also emit a poop-like scent to lure bugs.

9. Spiders don't have ears, but they aren't deaf. Instead, they sense sounds using strands on their superhairy bodies and legs.

10. Male wolf spiders "purr" to attract females. The gents rub two legs together to make dead leaves vibrate. The leaves make a purring sound, and the ladies sense the good vibrations.

11. Spiders pluck the strands of their webs and listen to the vibrations to determine where the weak spots are. Each strand is tuned to a different note, like strings on a guitar.

12. Wolf spiders make devoted mothers, carrying their egg sacs everywhere. After the spiderlings hatch, they hitch piggyback rides on their mother for several days.

13. Tarantulas are huge and bristly. And when they kick or flick those barbed bristles, watch out! The tiny hairs can embed in painful spots like eyes.

14. The Goliath bird-eater is one of the largest spiders, with a twelve-inch leg span. This tarantula pounces on birds, frogs, mice, and snakes.

15. The giant golden orb weaver munches on bats after the flying mammals get entangled in enormous five-foot webs.

16. Diving bell spiders use air bubbles to breathe underwater. They need to come up for air only once per day. Their silk bubble webs nestle among water plants, where spiders catch fish and insects.

17. Spiders wear their skeletons on the outside of their bodies. Since their exoskeletons don't grow, spiders need to molt by busting out from the inside until their old exoskeletons crack.

18. Spiders aren't royal, but they do have blue blood thanks to high levels of copper.

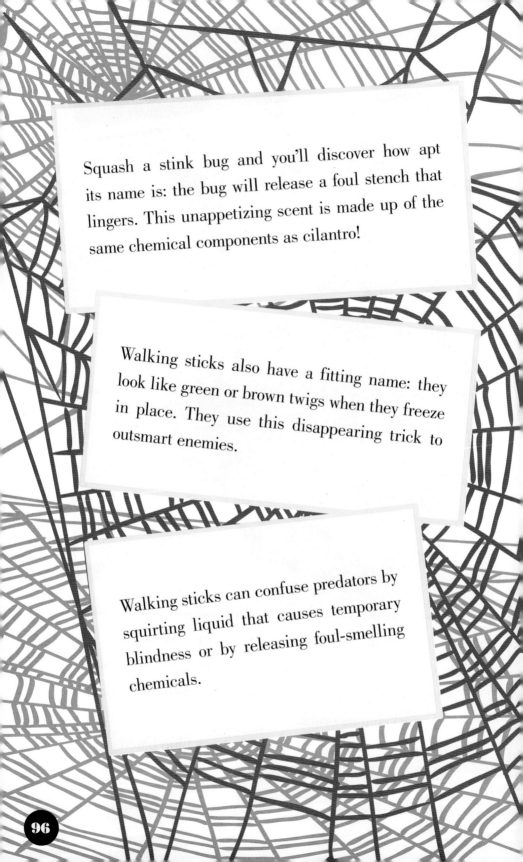

Squash a stink bug and you'll discover how apt its name is: the bug will release a foul stench that lingers. This unappetizing scent is made up of the same chemical components as cilantro!

Walking sticks also have a fitting name: they look like green or brown twigs when they freeze in place. They use this disappearing trick to outsmart enemies.

Walking sticks can confuse predators by squirting liquid that causes temporary blindness or by releasing foul-smelling chemicals.

Synchronous fireflies put on flashy displays every June in the Great Smoky Mountains. Male lightning bugs use flashing light patterns to court females. Thousands of hopeful suitors repeat the same pattern: up to eight flashes of yellow light followed by up to ten seconds of darkness.

Besides adults, firefly eggs, larvae, and pupae all are bioluminescent. They emit "cold" light, with nearly 100 percent of the energy given off as a bright, heatless light. It's as if they're carrying their own glow sticks!

Every thirteen or seventeen years, periodical cicadas rise up from underground, where they've been sucking up sap from plant and tree roots.

The cicadas are back in town, and they can overwhelm regions with up to 1.5 million emerging per acre! Then even predators such as birds and skunks become too full to gorge on this buzzing buffet.

With blood red eyes and ghostly white bodies that turn black, chunky cicadas measure two inches long.

Millions of male cicadas produce earsplitting sounds up to 100 decibels (being near them would be like standing three feet away from a chainsaw) to attract females.

Cicada wings have nano-scale spikes and a chemical coating that repel water and keep them free of bacteria. By studying the wings' complex surface, scientists hope to develop high-tech materials.

As dung beetles fly, they wave their antennae through the air to detect a specific smell: poop!

These beetles are picky eaters. They only dine on dung that has passed through animals that eat plants, like cows.

A male dung beetle can roll a gigantic ball of poop that can weigh up to fifty times his weight.

This hefty dung ball acts as an engagement ring. If the female accepts, the male rolls the ball while his fiancée rides atop it. The couple keeps a sharp lookout in case other beetles attempt to steal the ball.

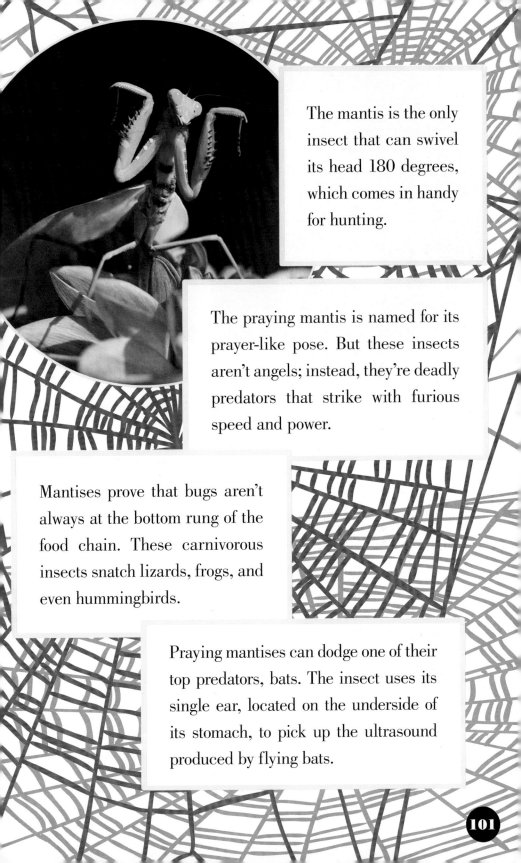

The mantis is the only insect that can swivel its head 180 degrees, which comes in handy for hunting.

The praying mantis is named for its prayer-like pose. But these insects aren't angels; instead, they're deadly predators that strike with furious speed and power.

Mantises prove that bugs aren't always at the bottom rung of the food chain. These carnivorous insects snatch lizards, frogs, and even hummingbirds.

Praying mantises can dodge one of their top predators, bats. The insect uses its single ear, located on the underside of its stomach, to pick up the ultrasound produced by flying bats.

Adult dragonflies grab insect prey with their feet as they swoop through the air. If they can't fly, they'll starve.

Each of a dragonfly's four wings can move independently. This flying insect uses muscles attached to the base of each wing to control wing shape and angle. Then the dragonfly can fly in all directions—up, down, forward, backward, from side to side—and even hover like a helicopter!

One species of dragonfly, the globe skimmer, migrates eleven thousand miles back and forth across the Indian Ocean. It has the longest migratory journey of any insect on Earth.

Dragonflies have had 300 million years to become expert fliers. These winged insects were some of the first to evolve. Fossils reveal that early dragonflies had giant wingspans up to two feet.

Dragonflies spend most of their lives in water as nymphs. There they pull water into their rectum to breathe through gills located there. When they need to move forward, they shoot water out of their rectum!

It's not easy being pink, as some grasshoppers discover. A genetic condition called erythrism causes an excess of red pigments. Predators gobble these rare grasshoppers since they stand out against green leaves.

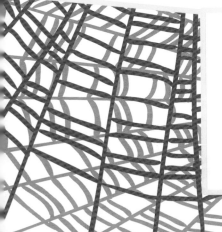

Grasshoppers' beefy hind legs resemble a bodybuilder's thighs. But if you could jump the way grasshoppers do, you'd be able to leap the length of a football field!

Greater wax moth caterpillars have a bizarre super-power: they gobble polyethylene. A chemical inside their digestive system breaks down this plastic, which is used in packaging such as grocery bags. Could they help us find a solution to plastic pollution?

The monarch butterfly's flashy yellow and orange wing colors warn off birds. If predators ignore the warning and take a bite, they're in for a poisonous surprise. The wings taste terrible thanks to the milkweed that the butterflies ate as caterpillars.

Patterns on the upper corners of the atlas moth's wings confuse predators. Instead of wings, startled predators spot two cobra snake heads.

Fruit flies have filthy habits. They breed in decaying plants and poop; they gobble blood, pus, and other animal fluids.

What do British soldiers' red coats and lipstick have in common? They obtain their color from tiny sap-sucking insects. It takes about seventy thousand dried cochineal insects to make just one pound of dye.

Arizona bark scorpions, the most venomous in North America, glow bright blue or green under UV light.

You now know 75 facts about INTRIGUING INSECTS AND SURPRISING SPIDERS!

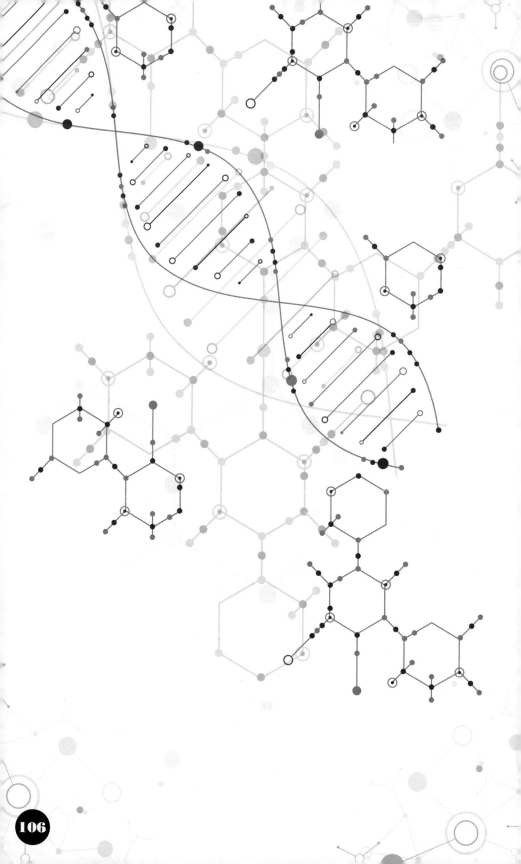

Strange Science

Listen closely: science has amazing secrets to share. All these facts might sound like science fiction, but they're nonfiction—true!

—

Earth is home to more than 391,000 species of plants, with about 2,000 more discovered every year. We've gathered some of the strangest for you.

1. Would you stand in line for hours to get a whiff of the corpse flower? Curious mobs flock to botanical gardens to sniff a putrid plant called the corpse flower. It smells like rotting bodies, dead fish, and sewage.

2. Besides having a powerful stink, the corpse flower is ginormous. It grows up to twelve feet tall with a flower measuring three feet or more in diameter . . . the better to smell! Thankfully it rarely blooms, and then only for a brief eight to twelve hours.

3. The pungent aroma and burgundy corpse flower attract bloodthirsty pollinators like flesh flies. Once lured inside the flower, they discover there's nothing to eat and fly away with pollen-covered legs.

4. The white baneberry is nicknamed doll's eye because of the shape of its fruit. But these "eyes" are toxic.

5. An ancient fruit called medlar is only ripe when it's rotten. Because of its strange shape, medieval Europeans called the fruit "open-arse."

6. The Venus flytrap is carnivorous. Its sensitive lobes snap shut to trap prey such as grasshoppers, ants, and spiders. However, flytraps don't eat the insects that pollinate them.

7. The purple pitcher plant also traps victims, including salamanders. It sends them down a deep cavity with downward-pointing bristles. There's no escape.

8. Sundew plants capture insects using red sticky tentacles. Then the leaf rolls around the prey to digest it.

9. Baseball plants are shaped like the ball with ridges that look like seams. This succulent plant almost went extinct due to poaching, plus the pod only contains two to three seeds.

10. Would you snack on the "bleeding tooth fungus" plant? It is edible, but the fluid on its surface not only resembles blood, but it also tastes bitter.

11. The wonderfully weird Welwitschia grows in the Namib Desert. Its two opposite leaves grow and grow and grow for the life of the plant—up to 1,500 years!

12. Lithops look like living pebbles. Their fleshy pairs of leaves are brown or gray.

13. One sunflower plant grown in Michigan set a world record: it had 837 heads!

14. The Peruvian apple cactus can tower thirty feet high. Its large creamy flowers open one night only.

15. The moonflower's trumpet-shaped blooms unfurl at night. The flowers curl up and close with the morning sun.

16. Night blooming flowers need to smell sweet so pollinators like hawkmoths can find them in the dark. Some moonflowers give off a lemon fragrance.

17. If you touch the orange jewelweed plant, its seedpods explode. Seeds soar through the air to survive in different spots. No wonder this plant has earned the name touch-me-not!

18. Besides spring-loaded seedpod, jewelweed is a natural poison ivy remedy. Just roll its leaves to release the oils and rub on your afflicted areas. No more itching!

19. Bananas grow on large herbs, not trees, which can reach heights of twenty-five feet. And that familiar yellow fruit is technically a berry.

20. Giant hogweed is the stuff of nightmares. This Herculean weed looks like Queen Anne's lace on steroids, growing up to eighteen feet tall. Hogweed produces toxic sap that causes severe burns and blindness.

21. Chocolate cosmos has velvety crimson flowers that smell like dark chocolate.

22. When Japanese farmers grow watermelons in glass boxes, the melons form into a cube shape. Because the melons are harvested before they're ripe, they are inedible and for decoration only.

The late Queen Elizabeth's cows get the royal treatment: waterbeds! These dreamy beds tailor to the cows' curves and put less pressure on their muscles.

What would your pet hamster do if you died? In a bizarre case, a free-roaming golden hamster created a new burrow using its deceased owner's skin, fat, and muscle tissues.

Now there are greener options than conventional burial and cremation for human bodies. An eco-friendly mush-room suit helps the body return to the earth. And human composting transforms a human body into several hundred pounds of soil.

John Duns Scotus believed that the wearing of conical hats would funnel knowledge from the pointed tip to the brain. This philosopher and his "Dunsmen" pals wore dunce hats to show that they were wise men.

Your brain is capable of processing images at super rapid speeds. Neuroscientists discovered that the brain could identify images that you view for thirteen milliseconds.

The largest snowflake ever recorded measured fifteen inches wide. That was in 1887 in the Territory of Montana.

Think oxygen is colorless? It is when it's a gas, but when it liquefies, oxygen becomes a blue fluid.

The Denmark Strait cataract is the world's largest waterfall, but you can't visit it. This waterfall is entirely underwater, plunging nearly two miles down. Underwater waterfalls occur when frigid water meets warmer water; the cold, dense water sinks beneath the warmer water to create a downward flow.

You also can't visit Guaíra Falls, once one of the world's biggest waterfalls. Made up of eighteen falls on the border of Brazil and Paraguay, Guaíra created a deafening noise that could be heard for twenty miles. But in 1982, the falls were submerged when a dam was built downriver to create a hydroelectric plant.

The bleach that transforms your gym socks back to white does expire. After six months, it starts to break down and become less effective.

Congratulations—you won the bubble gum–blowing championship. But yikes, that gigantic bubble exploded in your hair. Don't worry: massage a glob of creamy peanut butter into your hair and then comb out the gum.

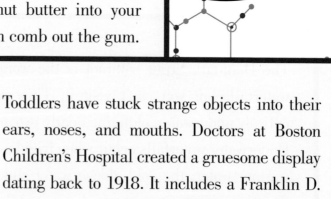

Toddlers have stuck strange objects into their ears, noses, and mouths. Doctors at Boston Children's Hospital created a gruesome display dating back to 1918. It includes a Franklin D. Roosevelt campaign button and carpet tacks.

Wouldn't you like to move to a location where it rains diamonds? Then pack your bags for Uranus and Neptune! Scientists used lasers to mimic the incredible pressure near the cores of these planets. Voilà: diamond rain in a lab.

Scientists estimate that there are more trees on Earth than stars in the Milky Way galaxy. Although an exact count is impossible, trees win with an estimate of 3.04 trillion trumping 100 billion to 400 billion stars.

A cumulus cloud looks light and fluffy, but it can weigh 1.1 million pounds. The weight of those water droplets adds up to about 100 elephants!

Some scientists believe that lightning strikes may have helped life emerge on early Earth. Intense heat and energy produced by bolts of lightning might have unlocked chemical elements and converted them into compounds essential for life.

People with illnesses can give off a certain scent: people with yellow fever have skin that smells like a butcher shop; those with diabetes have urine that smells like rotten apples; those with typhoid have an odor like baked bread; and people with a life-threatening metabolic disorder have urine that smells like maple syrup.

Researchers are developing an app to create the world's first poop image database. Their goal is to collect one hundred thousand poop photos from around the world to analyze how diet and lifestyle affects health.

And doctors are performing fecal transplants, swapping poop from a healthy person into a sick person's gut to treat a bacterium that can cause inflammation of the colon.

More people in the United States die each year from constipation—an average of 132—than shark attacks—an average of three.

Body farms sound futuristic, but they've been around since 1972. There, forensic scientists observe the decomposition of donated human cadavers as they decay outdoors. The different stages of decay are useful for police investigations and morbidly fascinating.

1. Within minutes to hours after death, rigor mortis sets in. The muscles go completely stiff before relaxing.
2. Gases pass through the blood vessels, causing the skin to turn a yellowish hue. At this stage, the skin starts to look like marble.
3. Bacteria get to work feasting on the dead body. Liquids and solids transform into gases such as stinky hydrogen sulfide.
4. Within a few days of death, the body bloats. It swells to nearly twice its previous size.
5. Gases force fluids out in a process called a purge or rupture event.

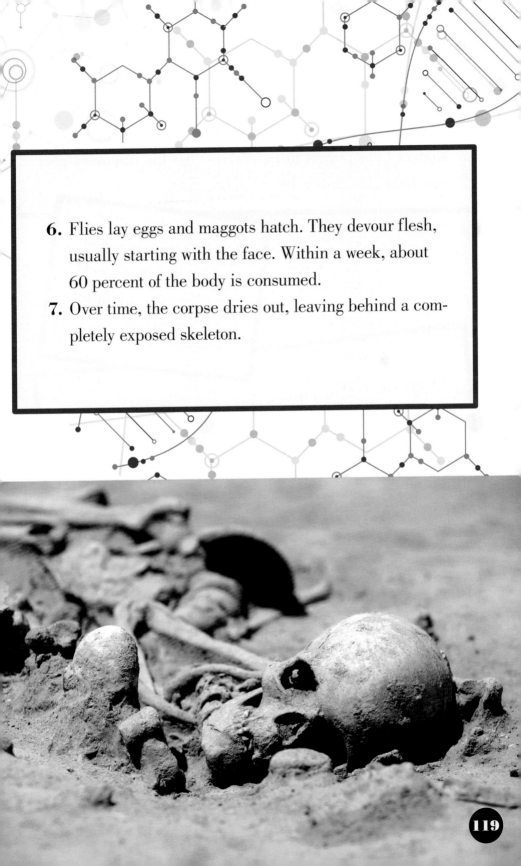

6. Flies lay eggs and maggots hatch. They devour flesh, usually starting with the face. Within a week, about 60 percent of the body is consumed.

7. Over time, the corpse dries out, leaving behind a completely exposed skeleton.

A schoolboy in Tanzania was laughed out of his physics class when he told his teacher that a hot mixture of ice cream would freeze faster than a cold one. Not only was the student later proven to be correct, but his discovery also now bears his name: the Mpemba effect.

There's also an inverse Mpemba effect: cold water heats up faster than hot water.

Water can boil and freeze at the same time. Under very specific conditions, the water freezes, then the frozen ice begins to boil, and finally it melts back into water.

If someone accidentally dropped a penny off the top of the Empire State Building, would it kill a pedestrian? No, cushioned by air, a penny would flutter to the ground at around 25 mph. Its effect would be similar to that of a leaf.

However, a ballpoint pen could turn into a lethal weapon if tossed from a skyscraper. It might shoot down like an arrow at 200 miles per hour, hitting someone's head with a huge force.

A beam of laser light can be trapped within a stream of water thanks to an optical phenomenon called total internal reflection. When the light travels through water, it's slowed down by the denser particles in water.

Animals sense Earth's magnetic field and use it to navigate. That's how salmon return to the stream where they were born to spawn, how female sea turtles return to the beach where they were born to lay eggs, and how homing pigeons make round trips without GPS.

Australian scientists discovered a gigantic detached coral reef in the Great Barrier Reef. This reef, the first to be discovered since the late 1800s, rises up 1,600 feet from the seafloor—higher than the Empire State Building.

One teaspoon of healthy soil contains more microorganisms than there are people on Earth.

About seventy countries around the world observe daylight saving time by setting their clocks ahead. However, this human invention has no impact on the sun's position in the sky or shadows it casts. You'll have to add an extra hour when you read your sundial.

The length of day and night is equal during the vernal and autumnal equinoxes. But there's no magical property on these two days allowing people to balance an egg or stand a broom on its end.

A glass crystal ball can be dangerous if it's placed in direct sunlight. Then the ball acts like a magnifying glass, concentrating sunlight strong enough to start a fire.

Researchers discovered a mega-penguin fossil in New Zealand. The 60-million-year-old gigantic penguin was the size of a man: about five feet, nine inches tall and weighing 220 pounds.

It's fun to watch milk turn a rainbow of colors when you eat a bowl of Froot Loops. This sugary cereal doesn't contain real fruit, and even more shocking, the eight colors all taste the same!

A Tree of 40 Fruit is a single tree that, through grafting, now grows more than forty different varieties of stone fruits. An art professor created this multifruit tree to be a sculpture and to keep unfamiliar fruit species from disappearing.

There's a name for that earthy scent you smell during a rainfall: petrichor. It's caused by plant oils that are released into the air when raindrops plop down.

Chile's Atacama Desert is so arid that it went five hundred years without rain.

Niagara Falls is shrinking due to erosion. The falls, which span the border between Ontario, Canada, and New York state, has eroded more than seven miles during the last 12,300 years.

You could dig a hole to China if you started at its direct opposite point: Chile or Argentina. But an ordinary shovel won't work; you'd need a superpowered drill to bore a hole through Earth's crust, mantle, and inner core.

Plastic bottles filled with water and two capfuls of bleach are being used as lamps. Invented by Alfredo Moser, the bottle lamps work by refracting sunlight.

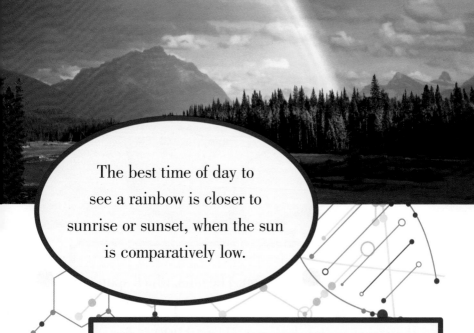

The best time of day to see a rainbow is closer to sunrise or sunset, when the sun is comparatively low.

More than 107,000 Americans of every age, ethnicity, and gender are on a national waiting list for an organ transplant. Every nine minutes another person is added to this list.

Most organs are donated after death, with donors ranging from newborns to seniors in their nineties. However, four out of every ten donations come from living donors, with the kidney being the most frequently donated organ.

Deceased organ donors can save up to eight lives. They can donate: two kidneys, a liver, two lungs, a heart, a pancreas, and intestines.

In 2017, neurosurgeon Sergio Canavero and his team transplanted a head onto a body, using two human cadavers. The eighteen-hour surgery is the first step in carrying out the operation on a living person, he said.

In 2021, researchers injected twenty-five human stem cells into the embryos of macaque monkeys. They created the first mixed-species embryos, known as chimeras, to determine whether monkeys might someday grow human organs for people needing transplants.

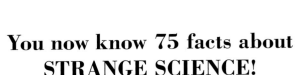

You now know 75 facts about STRANGE SCIENCE!

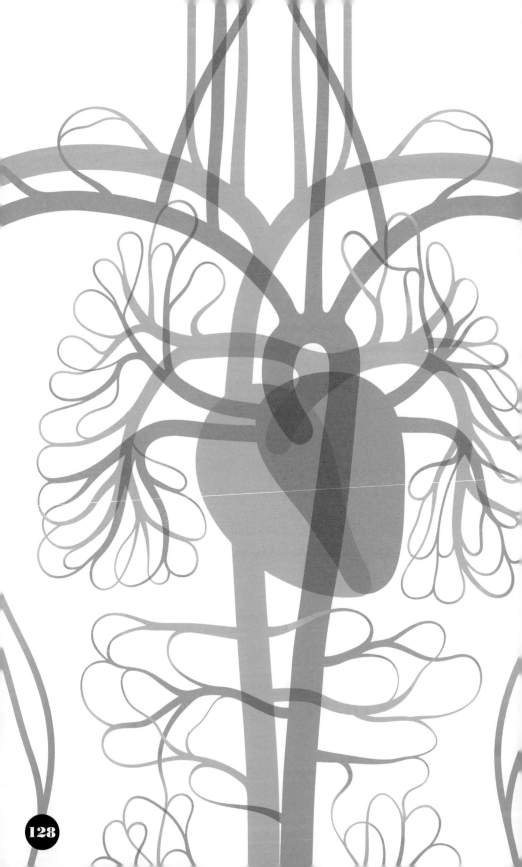

Your Bizarre Body

Your body is a marvel: complex and mysterious. It contains nearly one hundred trillion cells that allow you to do amazing things without even thinking. Let's explore some intriguing and weird facts.

—

Every day you're bombarded with sensory information. However, your body can adapt so you're not overwhelmed. This process is known as sensory adaptation. Which of these examples can you relate to?

1. When you first taste a certain food, your taste buds spring into action. The initial taste is distinct: sweet, sour, bitter, or salty. But after a few mouthfuls, the taste is not as strong.

2. Nonsmokers are bothered by the smell of tobacco, while smokers don't notice this odor. The same adjustment in smell occurs when someone applies fragrance. Within an hour, the wearer no longer smells the perfume.

3. Your eyes adjust when you go outside at night; the pupils dilate to let in more light. On the other hand, your pupils constrict when you step into bright sunlight.

4. When you jump into a cold lake or ease into a hot bath, the water might feel unpleasantly cold or hot. But your body will quickly adjust and adapt to either extreme of temperature.

5. Your ears adjust to the noise in your environment. Relentless city traffic or the sounds of a country meadow will fade into the background.

Humans have about 1.6 trillion skin cells, but you lose nearly one million every hour. Have no fear, they're constantly replaced with new skin cells.

Every year you'll shed more than eight pounds of dead skin. An average human can shed about 105 pounds of dead skin over his or her lifetime.

Your heart is a hardworking blood-pumping organ. Which of these heart facts surprise you?

1. Every twenty-four hours, your heart pumps up to 2,000 gallons of blood.
2. Kids have a heart about the same size as their fist, while adult hearts equal two fists.
3. Each year your heart beats about thirty-five million times. That adds up to more than 2.5 billion beats for an average lifespan.
4. Over the course of a lifetime, your heart will pump about one million barrels of blood—enough to fill three supertankers.
5. You have about six quarts of blood that circulates through your body three times per minute.
6. Your blood travels around 12,000 miles each day. That's about four times the distance across the United States, from the East Coast to the West.
7. All the blood vessels in a child's body stretch more than 60,000 miles, while an adult's measure around 100,000 miles.
8. You can feel blood moving on pulse points at your wrist or neck. When you place two fingers on these points, you'll feel the blood starting and stopping as it moves through your arteries.

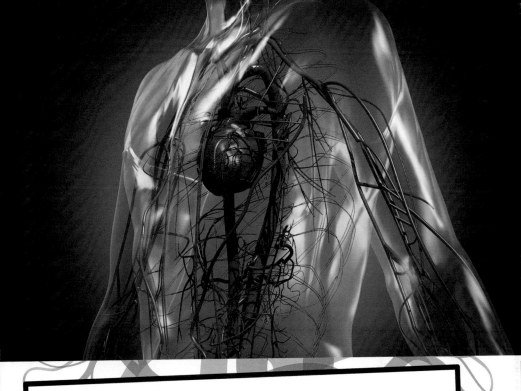

Do you hum along to your favorite songs? It's impossible to hum while holding your nose. Go ahead and try!

It's impossible to burp in space. Thanks to zero gravity, the gas doesn't separate from solids and liquids in your stomach. If you try to belch, you'll hurl vomit instead.

You can sneeze in space, but it gets super messy because there's no way to blow your nose while inside a spacesuit. Spacewalkers attempt to aim low off the helmet's windshield so their view can remain clear.

Wonder why our eyes clamp shut when we sneeze? This involuntary reflex sends a message to the six muscles holding our eyes in their sockets, making it impossible for your eyeballs to pop out.

If you do feel a sneeze coming on, let it blast out. If you try to block it, you might perforate an eardrum or rupture a blood vessel in your brain or one of your sinuses. Although these dangers are rare, are they worth the risk?

And just how fast does a sneeze travel? It can blast out of your mouth at speeds greater than two hundred miles per hour, discharging as many as forty thousand droplets.

A cough produces about three thousand droplets that rocket out of your mouth at speeds up to fifty miles per hour.

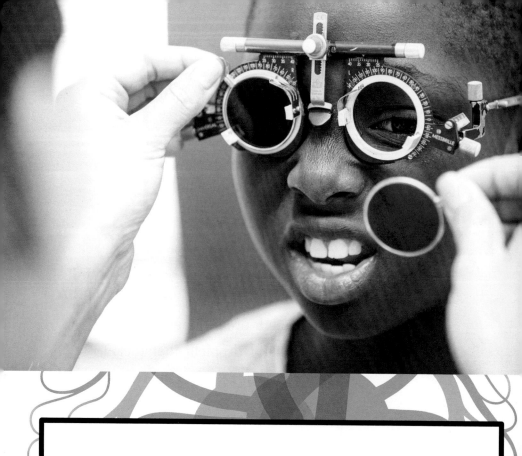

Males are more prone to color blindness. About one in twelve men have difficulty telling the difference between certain colors, such as red and green.

Bacteria and other microbes inside a human body are roughly equivalent to our human cells. Scientists calculate that we have about thirty-nine trillion bacteria to about thirty trillion human cells.

When you're embarrassed, your sympathetic nervous system reacts by increasing blood flow. Then not only your face turns red but also your stomach lining.

Does gum stay in your body for seven years if you accidentally swallow it? Nope, it rarely sticks around for more than a week before moving from your stomach to your colon and then exiting.

Can you drink too much water? It's difficult but not impossible, especially during intense training. Water intoxication can be fatal.

If you were adrift at sea and dying of thirst, it would be a deadly idea to drink seawater. The salt would cause your body to become dehydrated. Your kidneys would attempt to dilute this extra salt and you'd end up peeing out more water than you take in.

However, frozen seawater is far less harmful to consume because the salt forms separate crystals instead of squeezing into the ice crystals.

Opera singers, or anyone with serious lung power, can shatter glass. The voice will vibrate air molecules around the glass, causing the glass to vibrate itself to smithereens.

Just in case someone swallows a razor blade, science experiments show that acids in the human stomach can dissolve it after two hours.

How many senses does a human have? The standard answer used to be five: sight, hearing, smell, taste, and touch. Today, some scientists insist we have twenty-one senses, including balance, pain, and temperature.

Smell is the sense that triggers the strongest memories and emotions.

The tongue map diagram is wrong—you know, the one that shows sweet in the front, salty and sour on the sides, and bitter at the back. Instead, different taste receptors are found all over the tongue.

Toads might have bumpy backs, but they don't cause warts if you touch them. But the bumps on some species can ooze toxins that burn human skin.

Do you ever stay awake worrying about swallowing spiders in your sleep? Relax and get some shut-eye. These arachnids won't crawl into your bed or mouth; instead, they're far away hunting for prey.

It takes the average person ten to twenty minutes to fall asleep at bedtime.

You spend about two hours each night dreaming. Some people dream in vibrant color, others in black-and-white.

Your brain keeps score when you skip dreaming. Miss a few dreams from lack of sleep and it's payback time: your dreams will be action-packed and vivid when you sleep a full night.

About one in five kids sleepwalks regularly, but most children outgrow it. Only about 1 percent to 2.5 percent of adults sleepwalk.

People can do bizarre, dangerous things when they sleepwalk. One teenager climbed a 130-foot crane, walked across a narrow beam, and snuggled up on the crane's arm—all while remaining fast asleep!

According to a professor who measured his fingernail growth for thirty-five years, the nails on your middle fingers grow more rapidly than on the other four nails on each hand.

In rare cases, tonsils can grow back if even a tiny amount of tissue was left behind after a tonsillectomy.

Toddlers boost their brainpower by bombarding their parents with questions— an average of seventy-three per day. On the Top Ten list: Why is the sky blue?

For years, you've heard that urinating on a jellyfish sting will ease the pain. Not only is this a myth, but pee might also cause the jellyfish's stinging cells to release even more venom. Instead, use seawater to rinse off the tentacles.

Scientists in China used stem cells extracted from urine to grow a human tooth.

The bigger the brain, the smarter you are, right? Not so fast. Scientists say the relationship between brain size and intelligence has to do with the ratio of brain weight to entire body weight. So the average adult human's three-pound brain has a ratio to body weight of about 1-to-50, while the majority of mammals have a 1-to-180 ratio.

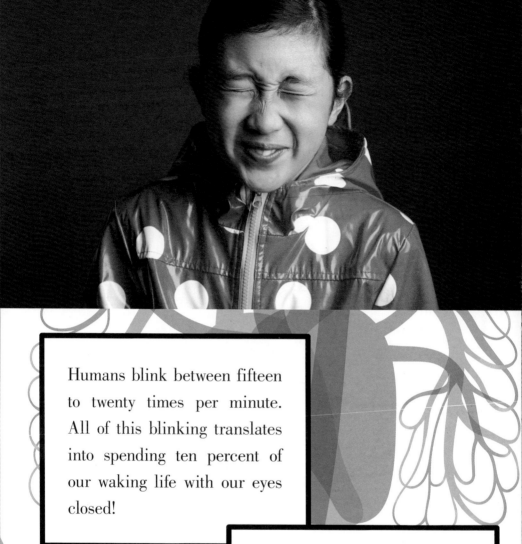

Humans blink between fifteen to twenty times per minute. All of this blinking translates into spending ten percent of our waking life with our eyes closed!

If you could count the strands of hair on your head, they would average one hundred thousand. Each hair will stick around between two to five years.

You'll lose between fifty to one hundred strands of hair each day, with women losing a higher number than men. Relax, this is a normal amount.

How fast your hair grows depends not on your sex, but on your race. Asian hair grows six inches per year; Caucasian hair grows five inches; African hair grows four inches. These numbers hold true for males and females.

Males start growing facial hair during puberty. If they decide to grow a beard when they're older, it will grow around a half-inch per month. Left untrimmed, that beard can grow three feet long.

Move over, fingerprints: these other body parts and characteristics are just as unique as you are.

1. Your iris—the colored ring around the pupil—has distinctive swirls and patterns formed in the womb. No two irises match each other, not even your own.

2. Unlocking a smartphone using an ear scanner? This technology is in the works. The bumps, ridges, and shape of your outer ears can identify you.

3. Bloodhounds know that each person's body odor has recognizable patterns. A sensor can detect a person's identity with an accuracy of 85 percent, although the dog's sense of smell still wins.

4. Your toeprints develop at the same time as fingerprints and they, too, have one-of-a-kind whorls and ridges.

5. Say *ah* and stick out your tongue. See all those bumps and ridges? They're uniquely yours.

6. Your teeth are also inimitable—that's why dental records can help forensic scientists identify Jane or John Doe.

7. And of course, DNA is still the gold standard. These biological building blocks are the blueprint that makes you unique.

Did you know that there are two kinds of tickling? Knismesis is a gentle sensation felt when someone runs a feather across the skin. Gargalesis produces uncontrollable laughter when someone targets a ticklish spot, such as the feet.

The stage before frostbite begins is called frostnip. Unlike frostbite, frostnip doesn't cause ice crystals to form in the skin.

A five-thousand-year-old mummy discovered in the Andes is the oldest documented case of frostbite.

What's the fattiest organ in your body? Did you guess the brain? This organ is made up of 60 percent fat.

Daniel Kish has been blind since he was a baby, but he has learned to "see" using human echolocation. With the same process bats use, Daniel navigates by using tongue clicks that bounce off objects to help him understand the space around him.

A patient in a coma with a severe brain injury was able to communicate through brain activity. The patient revealed to his doctor that he was not in any pain.

People who are struck by lightning get a skin reaction that forms fern-like patterns. Like temporary tattoos, these lightning burns gradually disappear.

James Harrison is known as "the man with the golden arm" for donating blood 1,173 times over sixty years. His blood contains a rare antibody that has helped prevent the deaths of 2.4 million babies.

A farmer in Iowa set a strange world record: he hiccupped nonstop for sixty-eight years! Doctors estimated that he hiccupped 595,680,000 times over his lifetime.

You begin life with 350 bones, but you end up with only 206 bones as an adult. That's because bones fuse together as you grow.

Babies are born with kneecaps made of cartilage. Kneecaps start hardening into bone between the ages of two to six.

Thanks to cartilage, an older person's ears and nose gets bigger every year. The cartilage breaks down and sags, leading to droopier, longer features.

If you saved up a lifetime of your spit, you could swim in it! One person produces enough saliva to fill two swimming pools.

Wonder why feet stink? Blame sweat. A pair of feet has five hundred thousand sweat glands that produce a pint of sweat per day.

The average person walks 7,200 steps each day. By the age of eighty, he or she will have taken more than two hundred million steps, or around 110,000 miles. That's enough to circumnavigate the globe five times!

Wisdom teeth usually appear between the ages of seventeen to twenty-five—much later than other teeth. About 35 percent of humans never develop wisdom teeth.

You now know 75 facts about YOUR BIZARRE BODY!

Weird Weather

There's no shortage of weird, fascinating, and unusual weather happening around the world. And to paraphrase Mark Twain, if you don't like the weather now, just wait a few minutes.

—

People have been forecasting the weather for centuries based on personal observations of the sky, animals, and nature. You've probably heard some of these weather proverbs, but are they fact or fiction?

1. "Red sky at night, sailor's delight. Red sky in morning, sailor take warning." There is some scientific validity to this saying. A red sky at sunset indicates high pressure moving toward you and bringing clear, dry weather, i.e., a sailor's delight. A red sky at sunrise indicates low pressure moving toward you, bringing clouds, rain, or storms, a good time for sailors to take warning.

2. "Clear moon, frost soon." When the night sky is clear, there's no blanket of clouds to keep the heat from disappearing back into space, causing the Earth's surface to cool rapidly. If the temperature drops enough on these clear nights, frost may form.

3. "A year of snow, a year of plenty." A covering of snow on fields and orchards prevents crops from sprouting and fruit trees from blossoming until the killing frosts are over. Then the melting snow provides moisture for a bountiful growing season.

4. "When the stars begin to huddle, the earth will soon become a puddle." When clouds increase, they hide whole areas of stars, making the stars that are still visible seem to cluster together. As the clouds increase, so too does the chance of rain.

5. "The higher the clouds, the finer the weather." Cirrus clouds—long, thin, and wispy—are high in the sky and usually seen during pleasant weather.

6. "When the bees crowd out of their hive, the weather makes it good to be alive. When the bees crowd into their hive again, it is a sign of thunder and of rain." Most bees forage for food from sunrise to after twilight, but if they suddenly stop to seek shelter, severe weather is on the way.

7. "Rainbow in the morning gives you fair warning." A morning rainbow indicates that rain is in the west and moving toward you.

8. "Mare's tails and mackerel scales make tall ships take in their sails." Their shapes describe different types of clouds: mare's tails resemble wispy cirrus clouds while mackerel scales are clumpy altocumulus clouds. Together, these two clouds mean a storm is approaching with high winds and the ships' sails should be lowered.

9. "Cows lie down when it's about to rain." Cows lie down for many reasons, such as to rest or chew their cud. There's no scientific evidence that a rainstorm is coming.

10. "April showers bring May flowers." Spring is the rainiest season, and April starts the growing season. Rain and warming temperatures provide flowering plants and fruit trees with nutrients necessary to thrive.

Folklore says if the brown stripe on a wooly bear caterpillar is wider than the two black stripes, the upcoming winter will be mild. However, if the brown stripe is narrower than the black, the winter will be severe. In truth, the width of the stripes depends on the caterpillar's age and diet. They don't predict what winter has in store for us.

Can a chirping tree cricket indicate the air temperature? If you count the number of times a cricket chirps in fourteen seconds and add forty to it, the sum will approximately equal the temperature in Fahrenheit.

Starting in 1886 on February 2, groundhogs like Punxsutawney Phil in Pennsylvania have been dragged out of their cozy dens during Groundhog Day celebrations. If these rodents see their shadows, according to legend, winter will continue for another six weeks. But predictions by these groundhog forecasters are no better than chance: Phil's only gotten it right 50 percent of the time the past ten years.

Misty drizzle falls much slower than rain. How many tiny drizzle droplets must combine to make one raindrop? The answer: about seven hundred.

There are eighteen hundred thunderstorms currently happening somewhere on Earth. That totals sixteen million storms in a year!

The typical thunderstorm lasts about thirty minutes and is around fifteen miles in diameter.

Severe thunderstorms produce large hail one inch in diameter (about the size of a quarter) or larger.

Big thunderstorms produce huge hailstones the size of softballs. These can rocket down at speeds faster than 100 miles per hour.

The largest hailstone recorded in the United States fell in South Dakota. This monster had an eight-inch diameter and weighed one pound, fifteen ounces.

Thunderstorms bring lightning—gigantic and dangerous discharges of electricity. Every second, more than one hundred lightning bolts strike Earth! Did you know these illuminating facts?

1. About four hundred people are struck by lightning each year in the United States. Most survive, but about twenty to fifty people are killed.
2. Fatalities have occurred during different outdoor activities: yard work, roofing, jet skiing, soccer, grilling, walking, and getting out of a car.
3. Lightning-strike survivors can have injuries including severe burns, ringing in the ears, brain damage, memory loss, heart problems, seizures, and personality changes.

4. You have one in three thousand odds of getting struck by lightning.
5. Most lightning occurs in the summer.
6. Lightning *can* strike the same spot twice. Especially dangerous are tall structures such as skyscrapers.
7. Since light travels more rapidly than sound waves, you'll see lightning before you hear thunder.
8. Calculate out how many miles away lightning is from you. First count the seconds it takes from when you see lightning until you hear thunder. Then divide that number by five. For example, if the difference is ten seconds, that means the lightning was two miles away.
9. Lightning can raise the temperature of the air around it to 54,000°F—five times hotter than the surface of the Sun!
10. If your hair starts to stand on end during a thunderstorm, this spells danger. Positive charges could be rising through you. Race indoors immediately.
11. The most electric spot on Earth is in Venezuela, at the mouth of the Catatumbo River. A massive stream of Catatumbo Lightning illuminates the night sky nine hours at a time. Lightning strikes about twenty-eight times per minute, equaling nearly 1.2 million strikes per year!

Why are most sunsets orange, red, and yellow? It's due to a phenomenon called scattering. Most of the shorter wavelengths of light—blue, violet, and green—are scattered away from your eyes. Then the longer wavelengths—orange, red, and yellow—pass through to your eyes.

Artists treasure the "blue hour" for its saturated deep blue that occurs at twilight. Then the sun sinks so far below the horizon that blue wavelengths rule the sky.

The "golden hour" is also called the magical hour for its warm, soft sunlight. This natural lighting is most common around sunrise and sunset, when the sun is close to the horizon.

Silver Lake, Colorado, still holds the US record for most snowfall in twenty-four hours, back in April 1912: six feet, four inches. By 32.5 hours, the snow totaled ninety-five inches!

Extreme snowfall in Capracotta, Italy, buried the village with 100.8 inches of snow in roughly eighteen hours.

What's so unusual about the date January 12, 2011? That's when forty-nine out of fifty US states had snow on the ground. The one holdout was Florida.

The town of Spearfish, South Dakota, gained fame for the world's fastest temperature rise. One January morning in 1943, the temperature rose from -4°F to 45°F in two minutes—an incredible forty-nine degrees difference!

Marble Bar is known as the hottest town in Australia, and with good reason. This outback town set a record in April 1924, where for 161 days in a row the temperature never dropped below 100°F.

Some weather is so bizarre that you wonder if Mother Nature is playing an April Fools' prank. Can you believe that these weren't hoaxes?

1. Dancing blue lights flickering from the rigs of ships during storms have mystified sailors. This phenomenon is called St. Elmo's fire—static electric discharges that mesmerize but don't burn.

2. Most blue moons are blue in name only. The term describes the second of two full moons in a single month. But sometimes the moon actually does take on that color. When ash and soot from forest fires and volcanoes mix with water droplets, they scatter the moon's light and give it a blue hue.

3. Snow in the Sahara, the largest hot desert in the world? It's astonishing and rare, but snow has fallen, spurring locals to slide down snow-covered sand dunes!

4. Fish and frogs tumbling out of rain clouds? Meteorologists say tornadoes that form over oceans and lakes can suck up small creatures and transport them via storm clouds. Winds carry these squirming loads miles away before dumping them.

5. Bizarre blood-red rain? Although it sounds like something out of a horror film, there's a scientific explanation. The rain doesn't contain blood, but minerals in desert sand that are whipped up and carried long distances before colliding with storm systems.

6. Other freaky crayon-colored rains and even snow are caused by precipitation tinged by nature or humans: yellow (pollen), black (coal mine dust), and milky white (dust).

7. Morning glory clouds look like massive snakes stretching up to 620 miles long. These unusual clouds form when sea breezes collide and create a tube-shaped cloud that sinks downward.

8. Lenticular clouds are shaped like round discs and form around hills and mountains. No wonder people mistake them for UFOs!

9. Most clouds form in rising air, but not mammatus clouds—they form in sinking air. These rare clouds look like giant white bubbles and give the strange sensation that the sky is falling.

10. Arctic Ocean frost flowers are spiky ice crystals that appear to bloom on the surface of polar oceans. Scientists have discovered traces of microscopic life inside the frost crystals.

11. You might think you're seeing triple suns, but the ghostly twins on either side of the sun are an optical illusion. These images occur when ice crystals in cirrus clouds refract the sun's rays.

12. "Water devils" rise out of bodies of water, tower at heights up to three thousand feet, and quickly slip back below the water. Could these whirling, noisy waterspouts have spurred sea serpent myths?

13. On the ground, "dust devils" whirl upward in rotating columns of wind. While most are short and brief, a few reach heights of three thousand feet.

14. "Fire devils" are dangerous whirlwinds that are spawned by wildfires. Ropes of fire rise rapidly and spin furiously.

15. "Snow doughnuts" look like gigantic frosty lifesavers. They form from a recipe of sticky wet snow, strong winds, and wide-open spaces.

16. Red sprites, blue jets, and elves sound like something out of a fantasy, but these bizarre flashes of colored lightning aren't imaginary. First spotted by pilots, these phenomena occur above thunderstorms and last milliseconds.

17. Imagine seeing your own shadow magnified and surrounded by a rainbow! To witness the Brocken specter, you'd have to be mountain climbing with the sun low and behind you and a mist below. Then your shadow will be projected in front of you through a heavenly mist.

Supercell thunderstorms can last for hours, travel dozens of miles, and spawn violent tornadoes. Below are eleven facts about these dangerously destructive forces.

1. The Tri-State Tornado in 1925 ripped through Missouri, Illinois, and Indiana. The longest and deadliest tornado in US history covered 219 miles in three hours and killed nearly 700 people.

2. The widest US tornado ever recorded had an enormous 2.6-mile width. It tore through El Reno, Oklahoma, in 2013 and was categorized as a rare EF-5 tornado—one that tosses cars and levels houses as if they were toys.

3. A tornado outbreak streaked across the Deep South from April 26 to 28, 2011, with a total of 343 tornadoes. On April 27 of that year, 207 tornadoes swept through nine states, causing 319 fatalities and 2,839 injuries.

4. Most tornadoes occur between 4 p.m. and 9 p.m. and last an average of five minutes.

5. Since tornadoes need moisture and warm air to form, they occur on every continent except Antarctica.

6. The United States has more tornado activity than any other country, with more than one thousand recorded each year.

7. Tornadoes develop more frequently in two regions: Florida and "Tornado Alley" in the Southern Plains of the central United States.

8. The first and only time Alaskans spotted a tornado was in 2005.

9. The safest spot to wait out a tornado is an underground shelter, such as a basement, or a windowless interior room on the lowest floor.

10. Know which weather signs to spot for an approaching tornado: greenish clouds and sky, a roaring noise like a freight train, a dark and low-lying cloud, and giant hail.

11. Thanks to improved weather forecasting and early warning systems such as radio station broadcasts, the tornado death toll has dropped significantly.

What are the most violent and destructive storms on Earth? If you guessed hurricanes, you're correct. These hurricanes are rated on an intensity scale of one to five based on wind speeds. The weakest, Category 1, has dangerous winds of seventy-four to ninety-five miles per hour. The strongest, Category 5, has catastrophic winds of 157 miles per hour or higher.

Major hurricanes, those rated Category 3 and higher, produce life-threatening winds.

The eye of a hurricane rises from the center of a storm like a chimney. The eye is the calmest part of the hurricane, with light breezes and a clear sky.

A ring of tall thunderstorms called the eyewall surrounds the eye. There, the strongest and most violent winds spin around the eye.

When hurricanes approach the coast, ocean levels surge up to thirty-three feet, causing devastating damages and deaths. Hurricane Katrina in 2005 was the costliest US hurricane, with damages estimated at $75 billion. About twelve hundred people lost their lives.

In 1953, the United States started giving hurricanes female names. Male names were included starting in 1978. Six lists of names are recycled every six years.

Names of catastrophic hurricanes, such as Katrina, are stricken from the list. Then the World Meteorological Organization selects another name as a replacement.

How much energy does a hurricane release? NASA says an average hurricane can expend a gigantic amount of energy equivalent to ten thousand nuclear bombs!

You now know 75 facts about WEIRD WEATHER!

Uncommon Pets

Most people share their homes with traditional pets: cats, dogs, or rabbits—the three most popular. Households with unconventional companions are on the rise, but remember: not all animals make suitable pets. Every state has exotic animal laws that restrict or prohibit certain types of animals.

—

What kid doesn't want a rodent? But think big: The capybara is the world's largest rodent, weighing up to 174 pounds. Nicknamed "water hog," the capybara requires a swimming hole.

Or think small: The tiniest rodent might only measure the length of your little finger. The jerboa uses long hind legs to jump as high as ten feet off the desert sand, so give this rodent plenty of space.

Another adorable desert animal is the fennec fox, which has oversize ears that can grow half as long as its body. Weighing two to three pounds, this fox is smaller than a housecat and can be trained to use a litter box.

Miniature donkeys should be kept in pairs because they enjoy each other's company. These gentle longears are easily trained. Although smaller than standard-size donkeys, they still weigh in at around three hundred pounds.

Pygmy goats are also scaled-down pets, weighing up to eighty pounds, that should be kept in pairs. But these escape artists need plenty of space and sturdy structures.

Playful potbellied pigs are smaller than farm pigs, but still grow up to 250 pounds. These superintelligent pets need stimulating activities so they don't become bored. Rooting boxes are a must for foraging.

With their soulful eyes and friendly dispositions, llamas make wonderful therapy animals. They do best with a furry friend sharing their barn and fenced pasture. Llamas can hike wearing halters and even sound the alarm when predators threaten the herd.

Alpacas are around half the size of llamas, with curlier and thicker hair fiber. Curious and intelligent, alpacas need companions. They warm up to humans who have earned their trust, but beware: an annoyed alpaca will hurl out a gob of slimy, stinky spit!

If you're a night owl, an African pygmy hedgehog makes an unusual and entertaining pet. These prickly companions are neatniks, and their large cages should be kept clean.

Sugar gliders are nocturnal pocket pets. They can glide up to 180 feet and learn different tricks. These marsupials love to climb and prefer tall cages.

High-maintenance chinchillas need their own AC or they'll overheat. These soft, plush rodents roll around in dust baths to clean their fur. Chinchillas prefer exploring to cuddling.

Degus are burrowing rodents that are active during the day. About the same size as guinea pigs, these adventurous pets love to explore and chew up a storm so they need plenty of safe toys to gnaw on.

Striped skunks enjoy playing, but before they are welcomed as pets, they need their scent glands removed. These curious creatures can get into mischief, so your house needs to be escape-proof.

Don't let those irresistible masks fool you—mischievous raccoons can get into trouble when bored. They're happiest exploring and playing in outdoor pens, where they can dunk their food in water bowls.

Coatimundis possess boundless energy, which they use to climb and swim. Inquisitive coatis need to keep their brains as active as their bodies. Wear gloves to protect yourself from their sharp teeth and claws.

Spiky porcupines carry a natural defense package: thirty thousand quills. These prickly rodents can't shoot these sharp spines, but the quills detach easily when a predator attacks. These "quill pigs" need chew toys since their teeth never stop growing. Handle with care, and make sure they're the only pet in your house!

Tamanduas are small, affectionate anteaters with a smelly spray four times more powerful than a skunk's. They can gobble up to nine thousand ants per day, but pets will eat sweet fruits, eggs, and cat food.

Kinkajous are furry golden mammals that live in rain forest trees, rotating their feet 180 degrees to grasp branches. Nicknamed honey bears for raiding bees' nests, these exotic creatures have a mostly fruit diet. Kinkajous who are raised in captivity can be friendly and playful but will nip when they feel threatened.

Elegant silver foxes are bred in Russia to have doglike personalities: they wag tails with happiness and bark. But you'll have to save every cent of your allowance to buy one of these domestic foxes—they have price tags up to $10,000!

Wolf dogs (like the one on the next page) are hybrids—usually either a gray or Arctic wolf mixed with a Siberian husky, Alaskan malamute, or German shepherd. While these cross-species mixes are photogenic, they come with many challenges. They're not house pets, so they need an acre of outdoor enclosed space; they are not eager to please, so they require special training. These escape artists need three to four hours of exercise daily.

Peafowl love to roam and browse on backyard bugs. A party of peacocks is happiest: one male peacock and several female peahens. They need a shelter big enough to fit the peacock's sixty-inch train of magnificent tail feathers. And beware: these exotic birds are incredibly loud, usually around dawn.

Stunning black palm cockatoos also make deafening calls. These bold parrots can live up to ninety years and require large aviaries. Although they can be a challenge, black palm cockatoos crave attention and can learn tricks and words.

Pekin ducklings are affectionate balls of fluff that can swim soon after hatching. These white ducks with distinctive orange beaks and feet are friendly, following people around like dogs. They'll need a secure coop and a spot in which to swim.

The Ayam Cemani is a rare ornamental chicken that's completely black: feathers, comb, beak, bones, organs, and meat. The only thing that isn't black is this unusual chicken's blood!

Underneath their thick, furry feathers, Silkie chickens have turquoise earlobes and black skin. These friendly chickens are polydactyl, with an extra toe on each foot—five instead of four.

While some people describe pigeons as rats with wings, others prize them for their navigational skills. One champion Belgian racing pigeon, named Armando, sold for a record $1.4 million!

These pets ratchet up the ick factor, so they're not for the squeamish.

1. Pets tarantulas such as the Mexican red-knee tarantula and the curly-hair tarantula make fascinating pets. But they're not for the squeamish because they require a live insect diet. Handle these spiders calmly; they might use their fangs to bite or spray you with barbed hairs when they get scared.

2. Another arachnid that feeds on insects is the scorpion. This is a pet you should observe rather than handle. Scorpions can sting, and a few species have venom that's deadly to humans. Plus their large claws can pinch.

3. The rosy boa is a popular striped snake that measures less than three feet long and has a docile personality. Although easy to care for, the boa dines on live rodents: striking, grabbing, and squeezing until the prey is dead and then swallowing it headfirst.

4. African giant millipedes have around one hundred legs and eat a vegetarian diet. However, if they get frightened, these arthropods will secrete a yellowish-brown liquid that smells repugnant.

5. Indian stick insects eat leaves and lettuce and can be tamed to sit on your hand. They don't attack or bite, but these insects need to be handled with care since they're very delicate.

6. The Madagascar hissing cockroach makes an unconventional pet. This hardy and huge hisser doesn't fly or jump, but it can scale glass aquarium walls. While this creepy-crawly roach doesn't mind getting its exoskeleton petted, it could get accidentally squashed if it escapes.

7. Praying mantises are masters of disguise: they can resemble leaves, tree bark, twigs, or even pink or yellow orchids! Plain or exotic, these insects are fierce predators, ambushing flies, crickets, and mealworms.

8. Despite their name, land hermit crabs need pals. They also need plenty of snail shells as they grow, molt, and trade up. Hermies love toys to climb over and hide in, but beware their pinching claws.

9. Don't kiss your pet snail (it can harbor parasites) or pick it up by the shell, which can damage the mantle and cause death. These noncuddly pets are interesting to watch. However, the humongous African land snails are considered one of the world's most invasive pests and are illegal to own.

10. Doodlebug is a cute nickname for antlion larva—a flying insect that stays in larval form for two to three years. This bug only walks backward so it looks as if it's doodling in the sand while building a pit. When an ant falls in, the doodlebug uses sickle-shaped mandibles to snatch its prey.

11. Male stag beetles have antler-like mandibles that they use for wrestling and battling other males. This shiny black

beetle is a popular pet in Japan, where, in 1999, a businessman paid a record $90,000 for a three-inch giant.

12. Ant farms, or formicariums, are fascinating to watch as these busy insects explore and tunnel. But make sure the habitat is well sealed: ants are excellent escape artists!

13. The red-bellied piranha has a reputation for being dangerously aggressive. These toothed fish grow quickly, so they need a large aquarium; if their tank isn't big enough, a hungry piranha might cannibalize one of his schoolmates. Don't dip fingers in the tank or you'll experience their razor-sharp teeth.

14. The tokay gecko will also bite fingers when threatened. This nocturnal lizard is an eager eater, chomping down on insects such as cockroaches and pinky mice.

15. Oriental fire-bellied toads have bright bellies that warn predators away from their toxic skin. Tiny pores secrete a milky poison that, while not strong enough to kill a human, can cause pain.

16. Some people keep crickets as pets, not just as feeder insects. Male crickets chirp using the comblike serrations on their wings. They're easy to raise in tanks, which must be cleaned to keep from stinking.

17. Mealworms are the ultimate low-maintenance pet—all they need is a bed of bran and some fresh veggies. These brown wormlike larvae of darkling beetles aren't slimy, but they do wiggle in your hands.

Searching for a cool dragon that doesn't breathe fire? Bearded dragons have spiny scales that make them look ferocious, but these gentle reptiles only grow up to twenty-four inches long. Colorful omnivores, bearded dragons eat a variety of insects and vegetables and are fans of misty showers.

Pacman frogs look as if they hopped out of the video game, with their chubby bodies and huge mouths. Like their namesake, these cute amphibians have giant appetites and will gobble up insects, guppies, mice, and even cage mates, so they need to be housed solo.

Flashy northern leopard frogs are bright green with brown spots. Powerful hind legs allow them to jump up to three feet. They require a tank with two zones—land and aquatic—with a secure mesh screen.

African bullfrogs have a reputation for being grouchy and loud croakers. And, surprise, they have sharp teeth and can and will bite! They chomp down on insects, small rodents, and other amphibians.

Ornate box turtles might nip when stressed, but once they become more comfortable they'll be your long-term pals for up to six decades. They plod along slowly but are expert climbers, so they require a high fence along with hiding places and spots to burrow.

Baby green iguanas grow rapidly—up to six feet long. They look like miniature Godzillas with spikes running down their backs. Adult need custom enclosures with branches to climb and heat lamps for basking. And iguanas' herbivore diet gives them amazing strength with tails that are powerful enough to break human bones.

Chameleons change skin color to signal their moods, such as calm, angry, shy, or afraid. These lizards also can rotate their eyes separately, allowing them to look up and down at the same time so they can nab insects with their superlong tongues. Be forewarned: chameleons are tricky to care for in captivity.

The axolotl looks like a tube sock with a tail. It sports feathered pink gills and a wide grin. People treasure these salamanders as unique pets, with the demand for axolotls surging after they starred in the hugely popular videogames *Fortnite* and *Minecraft*.

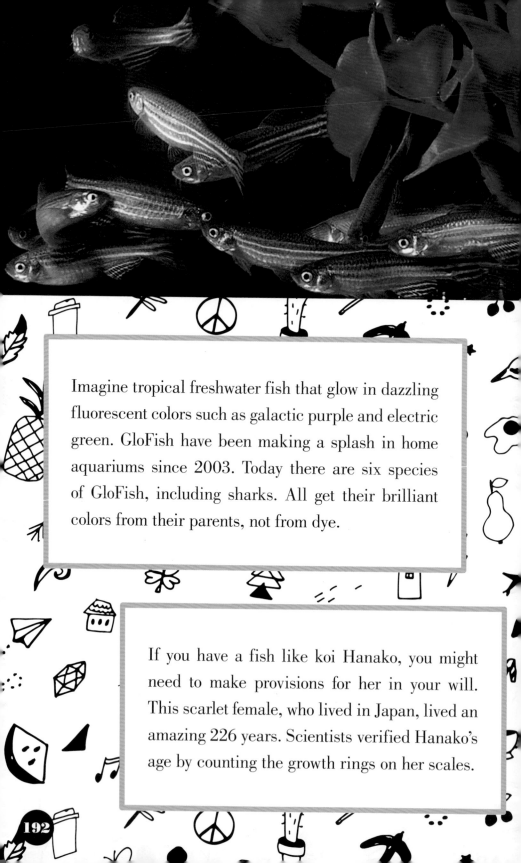

Imagine tropical freshwater fish that glow in dazzling fluorescent colors such as galactic purple and electric green. GloFish have been making a splash in home aquariums since 2003. Today there are six species of GloFish, including sharks. All get their brilliant colors from their parents, not from dye.

If you have a fish like koi Hanako, you might need to make provisions for her in your will. This scarlet female, who lived in Japan, lived an amazing 226 years. Scientists verified Hanako's age by counting the growth rings on her scales.

Pom-pom crabs clutch two sea anemones in their claws, waving these stinging predators both as self-defense and to stun prey. Tiny and colorful, the crabs make fun additions to saltwater aquariums with plenty of hiding places.

The California two-spot octopus is another fun aquarium pet. This friendly sea animal has distinctive blue spots around its eyes. You'll need a tank that holds at least fifty gallons and has a sturdy lid because the octopus will use its giant brain and the clever suckers on its eight arms to escape.

Sea monkeys sound exotic, and when kids spotted ads in comic books for these pets, they eagerly sent in their dollar bills. What they received were tiny brine shrimp with ultra-short lifespans. However, these "instant pets" did have long monkey-like tails. And sea monkeys did blast into space with astronaut John Glenn aboard space shuttle *Discovery*.

Lions and tigers and bears—oh, my! Many exotic animals are dangerous (either by attacking or spreading deadly diseases) and illegal to keep as pets, but that doesn't stop some people from owning them as status symbols. And once they're stolen from the wild, they'll never become truly domesticated.

1. Rare white lions Alpha and Omega were snatched from their mother as cubs so tourists could cuddle and photograph them. As the lion sisters grew, they were forced to take walks with paying guests. After the lionesses attacked and killed two people, they were surrendered to a protected natural habitat in South Africa.

2. Sumatran tiger cubs are adorable, but these critically endangered felines can cost up to $5,000. Unfortunately, in the United States, captive tigers outnumber those in the wild. And since a tiger can gobble up to eighty-eight pounds of meat in one meal, feeding one is an enormous challenge.

3. An orphaned Canadian black bear cub purchased for twenty dollars by a lieutenant during World War I became the inspiration behind Winnie the Pooh kids' books. The bear was donated to the London Zoo in 1914.

4. With their cobalt-blue plumage, hyacinth macaws are stunning, huge birds. In addition to screeching loudly,

these birds are classified as vulnerable on the list of
threatened species.

5. Alligators have powerful jaws built to crush bones and
smash skulls. These predators can grow to a whopping
one thousand pounds. Yet some people fight to keep
pet gators, such as Rambo, who wears clothes, "rides"
ATVs, sleeps in a bed, and dines at a table!

6. A pet Burmese python named Baby set a record as
being the largest snake in captivity, weighing 403
pounds. While Baby's keepers claimed she was a gentle
giant, pet pythons can overpower and strangle humans.
Otherwise, be prepared to feed rats, rabbits, and chickens to adult pythons.

7. Cane toads are gigantic, invasive, and poisonous to
pets unfortunate enough to nibble or swallow one. That
didn't stop a person in Sweden from owning a male
named Prinsen—the biggest cane toad on record,

weighing five pounds, thirteen ounces, and stretching fifteen inches long!

8. Intelligent capuchin monkeys have complex emotions. Raising one can be a challenge, especially as they grow more independent. These small primates are bursting with energy and become easily bored. They'll need a life-long supply of diapers (capuchins can live up to forty-five years), plus they scratch, bite, and fling poop.

9. In the wild, sloths spend most of their time hanging from trees, only visiting the ground once per week to poop! Behind their big smiles are ginormous sharp teeth that can puncture a hole through a human hand. These slow-moving mammals are three times stronger than humans.

10. The deadliest large land mammal in the world is (surprise!) a hippopotamus. Despite their enormous bulk—weighing up to five tons—hippos can move swiftly in water and on land. They kill around five hundred people every year in Africa, but that hasn't stopped a couple from befriending a hippo they named Jessica.

11. Foxes have wild manners: they're energetic diggers, they'll bite if you mess with their food or toys, and their toilet area smells like a mixture of skunk and ammonia. Despite these snags, domesticated red fox Juniper lives in a home with other rescued exotics and a doggy pal. Plus, Juniper is an Instagram queen with three million followers!

12. Opossums are the only marsupials found in North America. They're also extremely high maintenance and practically impossible to keep healthy in captivity. But one opossum is a rare exception. Rescued as a newborn from inside his dead mother's pouch, Bailey has bonded with his vet tech companion, and together the duo act as "possum ambassadors."

13. Would you want a king cobra for your beast buddy? A Malaysian firefighter has three deadly fourteen-foot pet snakes: King, Chip, and Cik Din. He's been bitten eight times and nearly died after ending up in a coma, but has no intention of giving up his dangerous, venomous snakes.

And if you're not ready to take on the challenge of an unusual pet, there's always the pet rock. Imagine, a pet that doesn't need to be fed or walked, bathed or groomed, and requires no vet visits. Plus the pet rock is easily trained to roll over and play dead!

You now know 70 facts about UNCOMMON PETS!

Ludicrous Laws

Every country has laws, but some are seriously ridiculous.
And you might be breaking one of these laws right now!

—

Here's an absurd law for each of the fifty United States:

1. Alabama: In Mobile, it's unlawful to sell or give away stink bombs or funk balls intended to create disagreeable odors.
2. Alaska: In Juneau, you can't take your pet with you into a barbershop or beauty salon.
3. Arizona: In Goodyear, it's unlawful to spit on sidewalks, in public parks, or inside public buildings.
4. Arkansas: It's prohibited to mispronounce the name of the state (which should be pronounced in three syllables).
5. California: If a frog dies or is killed in a frog-jumping competition, that frog may not be eaten or used for any purpose.
6. Colorado: In Boulder, ironically, no boulders may be rolled on city property.

7. Connecticut: Since 1948, a pickle cannot legally be considered a pickle unless it bounces.
8. Delaware: In Rehoboth Beach, no person shall pretend to sleep on any bench located on the boardwalk.
9. Florida: You have to feed the parking meter if you tie a camel, elephant, or horse to it.
10. Georgia: People may not keep ice cream cones in their back pockets on Sunday.
11. Hawaii: Coins are not allowed to be placed in one's ears.
12. Idaho: Cannibalism—willfully ingesting the flesh or blood of a human being—is punishable by imprisonment of up to fourteen years.
13. Illinois: In Galesburg, acrobatic or fancy riding of a bicycle, especially removing both hands from the handlebars or feet from the pedals, is prohibited.
14. Iowa: It's a misdemeanor to misrepresent margarine as a dairy product (i.e., butter).

15. Indiana: In French Lick Springs, all black cats must wear bells on Friday the 13th.
16. Kansas: In Topeka, it's illegal to toss snowballs or hurl stones at people, property, or trees.
17. Kentucky: In Fort Thomas, it's illegal for your pet to molest pedestrians or passing vehicles.
18. Louisiana: A person who steals an alligator could land in jail for up to ten years.
19. Maine: In South Berwick, it's illegal to park in front of Dunkin' Donuts.

20. Maryland: In Baltimore, it is illegal to bring a live lion into a movie theater.
21. Massachusetts: It's prohibited to dance to "The Star-Spangled Banner."
22. Michigan: A woman can't cut her hair without her husband's permission.

23. Minnesota: It's a misdemeanor to participate in any activity in which a greased pig is released for recapture.
24. Mississippi: In Natchez, it's illegal to allow your elephant to drink beer.
25. Missouri: In University City, it's against the law to honk someone else's horn.
26. Montana: Guiding an animal onto a railroad track with the intent to injure the train could get you a five-year jail sentence, a fine up to $50,000, or both.
27. Nebraska: In Lehigh, doughnut holes are not allowed to be sold.
28. Nevada: It's illegal to use x-rays to determine someone's shoe size.
29. New Hampshire: It's a violation to collect and carry away seaweed from the seashore at night.
30. New Jersey: Drivers are barred from pumping their own gas.
31. New Mexico: It's unlawful to permit livestock on public highways.
32. New York: A sliced bagel is taxed in this state, but not an unsliced one.

33. North Carolina: No bingo games shall last more than five hours.
34. North Dakota: In 1948, parking meters were banned.
35. Ohio: Operators of underground coal mines must provide an adequate supply of toilet paper.
36. Oklahoma: It is unlawful to promote or engage in bear-wrestling exhibitions.
37. Oregon: It's a misdemeanor to leave a container of urine on or beside the highway.
38. Pennsylvania: It's a misdemeanor to tell fortunes, including where to dig for buried treasure.
39. Rhode Island: Falsely impersonating an auctioneer is a criminal offense.
40. South Carolina: In Hilton Head, it's illegal to store trash in your car.

41. South Dakota: Farmers can set off fireworks or explosives to protect their sunflower crops from crows.

42. Tennessee: In Memphis, panhandlers must apply for a (free) permit before asking for money.

43. Texas: In Galveston, it's illegal to throw handbills, litter, or other objects from an aircraft.

44. Utah: You may not use any chemical, explosive, electricity, poison, firearm, pellet gun, or archery equipment to take fish or crayfish.

45. Vermont: Laws prohibiting the use of clotheslines are banned.

46. Virginia: In Chesapeake, anyone over the age of fourteen who engages in trick-or-treating is guilty of a misdemeanor punishable by a fine up to $250.

47. Washington: Killing Bigfoot, should you find it, can get you a one-year jail sentence, a $1,000 fine, or both.
48. West Virginia: It's illegal to hunt, catch, or kill wild animals or birds with the use of a ferret.
49. Wisconsin: Livestock such as cows have the right-of-way on highways.
50. Wyoming: By law, you must close a gate that crosses a road, river, stream, or ditch or risk a $750 fine.

There are strange laws to run afoul of around the world. Here are some of the top contenders:

1. It's illegal to feed pigeons in St. Mark's Square in Venice, Italy.
2. If you want to name your baby something other than the seven thousand approved names in Denmark, you need to get government approval.
3. Germany's Autobahn lacks speed limits, but you'll face a fine if you run out of gas.
4. Bringing chewing gum into Singapore is prohibited.
5. In the United Kingdom, it's illegal to hold a salmon under suspicious circumstances.

6. It's illegal to remove sand, shells, or stones from the Italian island of Sardinia.
7. Buying or carrying a counterfeit product is a criminal offense in France.
8. Defacing or tearing up the local currency in Turkey is an offense that could land you in prison for six months to three years.
9. High heels are banned from archaeological sites in Greece.
10. UFOs are not permitted to fly over, land, or take off in the French wine town of Châteauneuf-du-Pape.
11. In Finland, taxi drivers must pay royalty fees if they play music in their cars for paying customers.

12. Swimming pools and water parks in France ban men's swim trunks, requiring males to wear Speedos.
13. Selfie sticks are banned in the Italian city of Milan.
14. In Luxembourg, every car must have windshield wipers even if the car doesn't have a windshield.
15. It's illegal to hike naked in Switzerland.
16. Couples are banned from kissing in train stations in Manchester, England.
17. Climbing trees is prohibited in Magaluf, a resort town on the Spanish island of Mallorca.
18. If you get lost and stray down the wrong passage at a Paris Metro station, you'll be slapped with a fine.
19. In the United Kingdom, you'll be fined for riding in a taxi if you have the plague or another "notifiable disease" and haven't informed the driver.
20. Building sandcastles on the Italian beach of Eraclea is banned.

21. Winnie the Pooh was banned from being a playground mascot in Tuszyn, Poland, because the bear doesn't wear pants.
22. It's illegal to wear camouflage in much of the Caribbean.
23. In Victoria, Australia, it's illegal to fly a kite or play a game in a public space if it annoys someone.

24. Cambodia banned the use of water pistols during New Year's celebrations.
25. Swearing in public in the Muslim United Arab Emirates could get you fined, jailed, or deported.

26. People in Turin, Italy, who don't walk their dogs three times per day can be fined, and it's also a crime to dye a dog's fur.

27. In Canada, when you're making a payment of more than ten dollars, it's illegal to pay with more than one coin.

28. It's a misdemeanor to foul the air in Malawi (this refers to pollution, but one judicial official says the bill criminalizes farting to promote "public decency").

29. Portugal has banned peeing in the ocean, although it's unclear how this law could be enforced.

30. In Trinidad and Tobago, it's an offense to dry your laundry on any clothesline jutting over a street.

31. In England, it could be considered treason to place a postage stamp that bears the image of the Queen (or King) upside down.

You now know 81 facts about LUDICROUS LAWS!

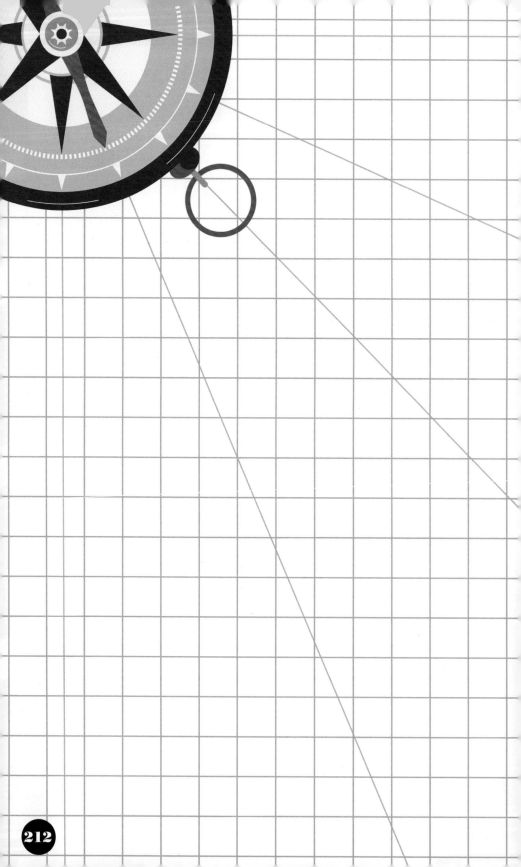

Extraordinary Places

There are astonishing places on this big blue planet that turn a trip into an unforgettable escapade. Take a preview on this armchair adventure—it's almost as exhilarating as being there!

—

Islands make strange and wondrous getaways. Which of these spots would be on your bucket list?

1. Why is a breathtaking island about ninety miles off Brazil's São Paulo coast uninhabited? Because "snake island" is home to about four thousand golden lance-head vipers whose bite can instantly melt human flesh and kill in under an hour.

2. Big Major Cay in the Bahamas also has zero human residents. But tourists are eager to visit. They flock here to photograph the island's world-famous inhabitants: swimming pigs!

3. Just Enough Room barely meets the criteria to be considered an island. A home and a tree are crammed onto the tiny speck of land, which is part of New York State's Thousand Islands.

4. Northeast Greenland National Park is the world's largest national park (375,000 square miles) located on the world's largest island. The park is an arctic paradise for polar bears and giant walruses, but it's nearly inaccessible with few visitors.

5. Nomans Land off the coast of Massachusetts is a paradise for spotted turtles and migratory birds. However, this picturesque island is off-limits to humans. It's littered with unexploded bombs from back when it served as a bombing range for the US Navy.

6. Felines outnumber humans six to one on Aoshima Island in Japan. A clowder of cats swarm this tiny fishing village, begging for rice balls from tourists.

7. Another island off the coast of Japan, Usagi Jima or Rabbit Island, is named for more than one thousand friendly feral bunnies. Some say the rabbits were brought to the island to test poison gas that the Japanese Imperial Army manufactured during World War II; others believe about eight rabbits were released by school kids decades later and rapidly multiplied.

8. Isola La Gaiola off the coast of Naples, Italy, is considered cursed because most of its former owners suffered either extremely bad luck or met untimely deaths. A small bridge connects the two islets, one with a crumbling villa and cobblestone streets.

9. One of Canada's most wild and remote islands can be reached only by air or sea, and visitors can only stay for one day. Wild horses and gray seals call Sable Island National Park Reserve home. The island has been the site of more than 350 shipwrecks caused by treacherous currents and fog.

10. Nature lovers from around the world visit Christmas Island, a rocky speck in the Indian Ocean, during the rainy season to witness 120 million red crabs marching toward the ocean to spawn.

11. Boldt Castle rises up from the romantic Heart Island in Alexandria Bay, New York. In 1900, millionaire George C. Boldt hired three hundred workers to build his 120-room dream castle as a Valentine's Day gift for his wife. But four years later, tragedy struck and the castle was never completed.

12. Another abandoned New York castle rises from Pollepel Island in the Hudson River. Francis Bannerman built his castle as an arsenal for his enormous collection of antique military equipment, including munitions.

13. Hundreds of creepy dolls hang from every tree on La Isla de las Muñecas in the canals of Xochimilco near Mexico City. According to legend, a resident of the island strung up the dolls to honor a girl who drowned in the lake.

14. A small rocky island in the Philippines is the geographical equivalent of the famous Matryoshka Russian nesting dolls. Vulcan Point is an island within a lake (Crater Lake) that is situated on an island (Taal Volcano Island) located inside a lake (Lake Taal) within an island (Luzon) in the western Pacific Ocean.

15. Venice is spread out over 118 small islands. Constructed on a lagoon in the fifth century, this city is supported with millions of alder tree trunks and connected by canals and bridges.

16. More than 150 islands make up Haida Gwaii in Canada. This 175-mile-long chain is pristine and isolated, giving the feeling that you've stepped onto the edge of the world. It's home to animals found nowhere else, like the Haida Gwaii black bear, with its hefty teeth that crack open crabs.

17. Elafonissi is an island in Crete that becomes a peninsula during low tide. Lagoons with warm turquoise water and sand that glows pink (thanks to millions of crushed seashells) turn this island into a picturesque paradise.

18. On the tiny uninhabited island of Staffa, off the coast of Scotland, is a sea cave famous for its natural acoustics, which cause ocean waves to echo. The hexagonal rock columns that form Fingal's Cave were caused by volcanic action.

These stunning out-of-this-world spots will make you question if you're still on planet Earth.

1. Giant's Causeway in Ireland looks as if a titan played a game of pick-up sticks with about forty thousand interlocking basalt columns on dramatic cliffs overlooking the wild ocean.

2. Glowworms only found in New Zealand light up caves in Waitomo with their blue-green bioluminescence. Visitors glide by boat through the Glowworm Grotto, passing beneath a galaxy of living stars.

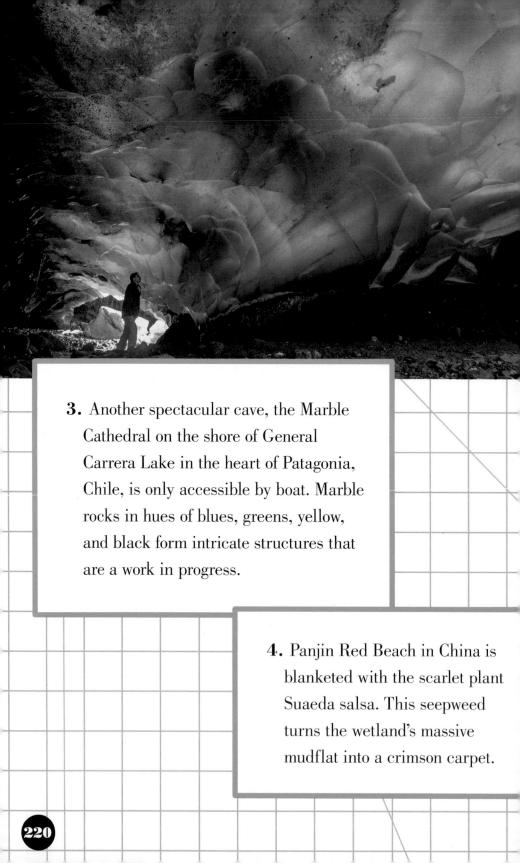

3. Another spectacular cave, the Marble Cathedral on the shore of General Carrera Lake in the heart of Patagonia, Chile, is only accessible by boat. Marble rocks in hues of blues, greens, yellow, and black form intricate structures that are a work in progress.

4. Panjin Red Beach in China is blanketed with the scarlet plant Suaeda salsa. This seepweed turns the wetland's massive mudflat into a crimson carpet.

5. Zhangjiajie National Forest Park's famous quartzite sandstone pillars tower toward the sky in Hunan, China. Its more than three thousand pinnacles inspired the floating mountains in the movie *Avatar*.

6. The world's largest salt flat, Salar de Uyuni, covers more than thirty-nine hundred square miles in Bolivia. On tranquil days, a thin layer of water covering the flat transforms it into the world's largest mirror, making it challenging to figure out where the sky ends and the land begins.

7. In the Mendenhall Ice Caves of Alaska, water flows over rocks beneath frozen blue ceilings inside a partially hollow glacier.

8. Dark evergreens form the mysterious Black Forest in Germany, which set the scene for many fairy tales by the Brothers Grimm.

9. A forest of giant natural crystals grows inside Cave of Crystals, part of Mexico's Naica Mine. Miners discovered this magical cavern in 2000, but deadly 120°F temperatures mean few can view crystals the size of redwood trees.

10. Zhangye Danxia National Park in China boasts rainbow hills that resemble a layer cake. Brilliant deposits of red sandstone and other minerals occurred over twenty-four million years to shape this colorful landform.

11. Colombia's Caño Cristales river resembles a liquid rainbow. But this vibrant display of colors—green, yellow, red, blue, orange, purple—isn't magic; it's caused by an aquatic plant, plus water and weather conditions.

12. Eisriesenwelt, which translates to "World of Ice Giants," is the world's largest ice cave. Tucked away inside the Hochkogel Mountain in Austria, the limestone cave stuns visitors with ice figures, gigantic towers, and frozen waterfalls.

13. Japan's Ryūsendō Cave features an underground river and four lakes, but the highlight is viewing platforms where visitors can spot rare and protected species of bats hanging from the cave's ceiling.

14. Giant Saguaro cacti tower fifty feet high and weigh more than ten tons. Visitors to Saguaro National Park in Arizona are treated to breathtaking vistas, desert sunsets, and the nation's largest cacti.

15. The largest yellow waterfalls in the world thunder down from a high vertical drop on the mighty Yellow River. The Hukou Waterfall in China gets its yellow hue from river sediment.

16. The Sea of Stars shimmers in the inky-black night waters of the Indian Ocean. Bioluminescent sea plankton causes this natural phenomenon in the Maldives. As waves break, plankton glows an electric blue so the sea appears to be full of stars.

17. The Great Blue Hole off the coast of Belize is a massive underwater sinkhole. This deep sapphire circular hole is nearly 1,000 feet across and 410 feet deep.

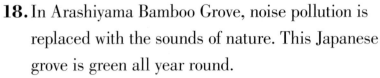

18. In Arashiyama Bamboo Grove, noise pollution is replaced with the sounds of nature. This Japanese grove is green all year round.

19. Estimated to be 130 million years old, the Borneo Lowland Rain Forest is home to a wealth of biodiversity. More than 15,000 species of flowering plants, 3,000 species of trees, 221 species of terrestrial animals, and 420 species of birds call this tropical rain forest home.

20. Great Bear Rainforest in British Columbia, Canada, contains stunning landscapes: four-thousand-foot-tall granite cliffs, fjords, waterfalls, and enormous cedar trees.

21. A purple carpet of bluebells carpets Belgium's Hallerbos Forest each spring, turning it into a fairyland.

22. You can touch the clouds in the Monteverde Cloud Forest Preserve. Located on Costa Rico's Tilarán mountain range, the forest is one of the most orchid-rich spots on Earth, with more than five hundred species.

23. Sculpted by wind and water during the Jurassic Age, the Wave in Arizona is an awesome sandstone formation. Its rippling lines and swirling colors give it the appearance of a dramatic ocean wave.

24. Lake Hillier in Australia contains water the color of pink bubble gum. This color pops in comparison to the neighboring bright blue Pacific Ocean. The source of the color remains a mystery.

25. Triple volcanic crater lakes of Mount Kelimutu in Indonesia change colors, with each lake turning a different hue.

Some spooky locations are hauntingly mysterious, where the strange and unexplained give visitors goosebumps.

1. The Pine Barrens in New Jersey span more than a million acres of unworldly beauty. It's home to creepy abandoned villages and allegedly haunted by the Jersey Devil—a creature with hooves, bat wings, and a forked tail.

2. An eerie decay has taken over North Brother Island. This twenty-two-acre island just off the coast of Manhattan once was home to "Typhoid Mary" Mallon and other patients with contagious diseases, but today birds are the only inhabitants.

3. Area 51 in Nevada is a top-secret military Air Force base used as a flight-testing facility where the U-2 spy plane was built. Surrounded by barren desert, this site spawned many reports of UFO sightings.

4. Unexplained disappearances of planes and ships in the Atlantic Ocean's Bermuda Triangle continue to be blamed on everything from aliens to sea monsters to time warps.

5. Dubbed "the Bermuda Triangle of Transylvania," Hoia-Baciu Forest in Romania has eerie vegetation and unexplained phenomena. Some believe the forest is a portal that causes visitors to disappear.

6. A bright red lake in Tanzania is the world's most caustic body of water. The sodium bicarbonate in Lake Natron turns unfortunate animals into stone statues and completely mummifies them.

7. Blood Falls looks like blood gushing down five stories out of the Taylor Glacier in Antarctica. But the grisly color actually comes from salty water rich in iron that oozes out from a fissure in the glacier.

8. Hundreds of peculiar pine trees grow in the Crooked Forest in Poland. The trees in this uncanny forest were planted in the 1930s and grew with a 90-degree bend at their bases, making them look like giant fish hooks.

9. When the arch of Devil's Bridge in Germany is reflected in the water, it creates the illusion of a complete circle. Legends claim that a devilish helper constructed the stone bridge in the 1860s.

10. Devil's Tower rises 1,267 feet above the Belle Fourche River in Wyoming, which challenges climbers with hundreds of parallel cracks that divide the tower into hexagonal columns. The stone tower became famous when it was featured in the sci-fi movie *Close Encounters of the Third Kind.*

11. The fiery Door to Hell is a 230-foot-wide crater in the desert of northern Turkmenistan. In 1971, after a Soviet natural gas drilling mishap, scientists set the crater on fire to stop the spread of dangerous gases. They thought it would burn out in a few hours, but fifty years later the inferno of flames still burns.

12. One lone flame burns underneath Eternal Flame Falls in New York. A natural gas pocket causes this strange orange-red light. When the flame sputters out, hikers relight it.

13. Millions of fairy circles pockmark the Namibian desert. These bare patches surrounded by rings of grass range in size from six to forty feet. Scientists are still trying to solve the fairy circles mystery.

14. Aokigahara Forest in Japan is nicknamed "suicide forest"; it's the second most common site for suicides after the Golden Gate Bridge. According to Japanese mythology, demons haunt this eerie, dense forest, where sound is muffled and hikers get lost.

15. The bizarre Dragon's Blood Forest grows on the remote island of Socotra, off the coast of Yemen. Here, the otherworldly cinnabar trees look like inverted umbrellas and bleed eerie bright red sap.

16. Epping Forest in England is an ancient woodland filled with nearly fifty-five thousand creepy old trees with bulbous trunks. It was once a notorious hideout for highwaymen, and it continues to be a burial spot for murder victims.

17. Red sand dunes tower over Dead Vlei in Namibia. Dehydrated camel thorn trees, more than one thousand years old and scorched black by the sun, form a forbidding forest.

18. Bright blue lava erupts from Kawah Ijen Volcano on the island of Java. As the lava flows down this active volcano, it creates a series of electric blue flames. The crater lake at the summit is a stunning turquoise, the result of its extreme acidity, which is close to battery acid.

19. The water in Lake Abraham in Alberta, Canada, shimmers turquoise in warmer months. In winter, the frozen water holds white bubbles that resemble snowballs. But this isn't Christmas magic—the lake has a bad case of (methane) gas trapped in the bubbles.

20. Loch Ness in Scotland is famous for sightings of Nessie—a mythical sea serpent. Although this monster's existence has never been proven, visitors continue to scan this deep-water lake hoping for a glimpse.

21. Magnetic Hill in India is an optical illusion—the road appears to slope uphill against gravity, but it actually slopes downhill. Local legends hold that this hill leads people to heaven.

22. The Moeraki Boulders are enormous spherical rocks that formed sixty million years ago, giving the New Zealand coast an alien landscape. According to Maori legend, the boulders are the remains of water gourds that washed ashore after a storm shipwrecked their ancestors' canoe.

23. Death Valley is the hottest, driest, and lowest national park in America. The Racetrack, a dry lake bed within the park, is famous for hundreds of rocks weighing up to seven hundred pounds that appear to have been pushed or dragged. Scientists finally solved the mystery: the rocks move thanks to a rare winter combination of ice sheets and wind.

You now know 66 facts about EXTRAORDINARY PLACES!

Phenomenal Fashions

Fashions allow you to express yourself. At a glance, what you wear creates a wordless means of communication. The only thing certain about fashion is that trends constantly change.

—

Strange fashion trends throughout history might cause us to wonder: What were they thinking? Some of these fads were fatal.

1. When a German dye company created an emerald-green shade, it became all the rage in Victorian times. But this vivid green clothing was deadly thanks to arsenic in the dye.

2. Women who wore the high-platform shoes called chopines needed attendants to help them balance. Some of these sixteenth-century footwear soared to dangerously dizzy heights of twenty inches!

3. To fit into tiny three-inch lotus shoes, young Chinese girls had their feet wrapped with bindings. Mothers broke their daughters' toes and then wound bandages to force the toes underneath the foot so the front and back touched.

4. In the 1850s, steel-cage crinolines created volume beneath popular hoop skirts. These could spread out to a circumference of up to six yards.

5. A codpiece was a pouch designed to cover a man's crotch and to store small items like money. Its modern counterparts are the jockstrap and the man purse.

6. The "macaroni" trend had nothing to do with pasta. Instead, it was a men's fashion craze that included sky-high powdered wigs with tiny hats on top.

7. Women wore towering French hairstyles called fontanges. Curls were piled into twelve-inch-tall wire frames and decorated with lace, ribbons, feathers, flowers, and jewels.

8. Beaver-fur top hats were groomed with mercury to make them look as glossy as silk. Unfortunately, mercury poisoning caused hat makers to exhibit psychotic behavior like the Mad Hatter in *Alice's Adventures in Wonderland*.

9. Large starched ruffs encircled necks. These accordion-shaped collars advertised the wearer's status—the larger they were, the greater the wealth. But they made it difficult to perform everyday activities such as eating and walking.

10. Since the hobble skirt was cinched at the ankles, women could only take tiny, dainty steps without breaking their legs. Ironically, this trend took place during the women's suffrage movement.

11. In Japan, women dyed their teeth black, a practice known as *ohaguro*, to complement their rice-powdered white faces. They coated their teeth with iron and spices dissolved in vinegar.

12. Tight Victorian corsets gave women a curved hourglass figure. These undergarments were stiffened by whalebone and tightened by laces, which squashed internal organs and made breathing difficult.

13. Elongated skulls made ancient Mayan nobility stand out. An infant's head was bound with bandages and small boards until the artificially deformed skull had a particular shape.

14. Women in several tribes of Southeast Asia and Africa still practice the ancient custom of neck stretching. Starting around age five, they wear coils of heavy brass rings, with more added over time. But the elongated neck is an illusion: the pressure of the coils pushes down on the rib cage until the collarbones appear to be part of the neck.

15. Scarification is one of the oldest forms of body art. In many cultures, intricate designs are cut into the skin during rituals, leaving behind raised scars.

16. In the seventeenth and eighteenth centuries, men wore powdered wigs to cover up baldness. Since few people bathed, the wigs were scented with lavender or orange to conceal body odor. Periodically, men sent their hairpieces to a wigmaker to be deloused.

17. During the seventeenth century, plague doctors wore bird masks with long beaks.

These were stuffed with dried flowers, spices, and herbs to battle harmful fumes that they mistakenly believed spread the plague. Today, people wear bird masks to masquerade balls.

18. Stylish women in the 1500s wore gruesome accessories. A zibeline consisted of the entire pelt of a small animal, such as a sable, worn draped at the neck. Gold or silver heads and paws, plus jeweled eyes, adorned the pelts. Fleas were supposed to bite the zibeline, but the bugs preferred warm living bodies.

19. Another macabre fashion trend around 150 years ago featured wearable taxidermy. Entire stuffed birds perched on women's hats. Hunters killed hundreds of thousands of birds, nearly causing some, such as snowy egrets, to become extinct.

20. Ancient Egyptians wore dark kohl around their eyes. This eye makeup acted as a natural sunblock, similar to the eye black under sports figures' eyes. Despite containing lead, the kohl also kept bacterial infections out of Egyptians' eyes.

21. During the Great Depression, women transformed flour sacks into clothing out of necessity. These DIY dresses turned thrifty women into 1930s fashionistas.

22. Distressed jeans, with their already-worn look, remain popular. However, the workers who sandblast denim can get lung disease caused by inhaling silica dust from the sand.

23. High heels seem to add inches to your height and can elongate your legs, but those killer stilettos also damage and deform feet and cause sprained ankles.

24. A US footwear company caused outrage with its line of high-heeled shoes designed for infants up to six months old. Ads describe the shoes, which have collapsible heels and pointed toes, as "diva defining."

25. Eyeball tattooing, where the whites of eyes are filled in with colored ink, is a dangerous trend with a real risk of vision loss.

26. Another hazardous trend entails surgically implanting jewelry in the eyeball. The doctor makes a tiny slit in the membrane covering the white part of the eye and inserts a platinum shape such as a star.

27. People have been piercing their ears, lips, noses, and tongues and attaching rings and studs for thousands of years. Some people are taking body modification a step farther and getting their tongues forked, splitting them from the tip to the back for up to two inches.

28. Dissolvable garments will be the final fashion statement people make. The biodegradable fibers are designed to disintegrate along with the body.

Fashion can be influenced by culture: newspapers and magazines, TV and movies, music and books. Cultural icons famous for their style have a big impact on what people wear.

1. When Madonna danced onstage during her Blond Ambition Tour in 1990, she wore a pink satin bullet bra. The singer wore this underwear as outerwear, but fashionable women wore the original sharply pointed bras under their clothes in the 1940s and 1950s.

2. Dark sunglasses are an important part of a secret agent's uniform. Sales of the Ray-Ban sunglasses worn by the main characters in *Men in Black* zoomed after the film's release.

3. Dubbed "unicorn armpit hair," dyed rainbow body hair is a trend against society's beauty standards for women. This colorful look racked up views on social media.

4. Colorful photos of men channeling their inner "merman"— dying their hair and beards in vivid blues, greens, and purples—also popped up on social media.

5. Elvis Presley's flamboyant stage costumes bent strict gender rules of the 1950s and inspired other men to have fun with fashion.

6. The Beatles' mod mop-top haircuts of the early 1960s created a sensation when the four heartthrobs appeared on *The Ed Sullivan Show*.

7. French designer Louis Réard created the bikini in 1946 using thirty inches of fabric. This scandalously skimpy swimsuit became an instant hit.

8. The "little black dress" designed by Coco Chanel in 1926 never went out of style. It gained a new allure when Audrey Hepburn wore her iconic black sheath dress with an elaborate pearl necklace in the 1961 film *Breakfast at Tiffany's.*

9. Hemlines rose upward in the 1960s, with some daringly short miniskirts escalating to eight inches above the knees.

10. Pop art influenced fashion in the mid-1960s. Artist Andy Warhol's *Campbell's Soup Cans* appeared on a paper dress.

11. The disco dance craze reached new heights when *Saturday Night Fever* was released in 1977. When John Travolta donned his three-piece white suit and preened in front of mirrors, men around the world imitated him.

12. White wool togas worn in ancient Rome were elaborately draped in folds and pleats; enslaved people helped dress the wearer. College students held toga parties after the one immortalized in the 1978 film *Animal House.*

13. The human body is a blank canvas, and people from many cultures have been decorating their bodies with tattoos throughout history. Today, tattoos have become mainstream with more than one-quarter of Americans expressing themselves through ink.

14. Body artist Joel Alvarez uses black and metallic electrical tape to create barely there swimsuits.

15. American rapper M. C. Hammer wore billowy pants onstage. Hammer's outlandish pants resembled the harem trousers worn thousands of years ago in India, Iran, and Turkey.

16. Bell-bottoms were a unisex fashion craze in the 1960s, but sailors had worn pants with flared legs for centuries. These practical pants could be rolled up while seamen swabbed the decks, and the belled legs inflated with air if a sailor fell overboard.

17. The punk music scene inspired spiky hair and colorful mohawks, ripped black clothes with chains and metal studs, safety pin piercings, and dog collars.

18. Goth, the dark fashion trend that emerged from the 1980s punk scene, includes black vampirish clothing, heavy eyeliner, blood-red lipstick, black nail polish, and chunky silver crosses.

19. Cool, colorful leggings became popular during the aerobics craze of the 1980s, with exercise-video star Jane Fonda leading the way.

20. The world's most expensive lingerie was modeled in a fashion show. The bra and panties featured around three thousand diamonds and twenty-two rubies and boasted a hefty $15 million price tag.

21. The media promoted gender-specific colors back in the early 1900s: pink for boys and blue for girls. No, that's not a typo; red (used to create the pale tint of pink) was considered too harsh for girls. In the 1940s, the color assignments were switched.

22. The rainbow flag made its first appearance at the 1978 San Francisco Gay Freedom Parade. Today, the six-colored flag continues to fly, symbolizing LGBTQ+ pride.

23. Cosplay started at science-fiction conventions, where cosplayers dressed up in costumes to emulate fictional characters from comic books, movies, and video games. Some cosplayers also adopt their characters' body language and mannerisms to bring this art form to life.

24. You've seen photos of celebrities carrying miniature dogs in big purses. But the trend of tiny pets as fashion accessories goes way back. Women in ancient Rome stuffed their Maltese dogs in their sleeves, and in ancient China, men carried their Pekinese lapdogs inside their robes.

25. Fascinators, those elaborate clip-on headpieces worn at formal events, date back to the late 1800s. They surge in popularity every time that Kate Middleton, the Princess of Wales, wears her chic headwear.

26. White wedding gowns became traditional after Queen Victoria wore one at her 1840 wedding to Prince Albert. Prior to that, brides wore colored dresses, including blue and black.

27. After Prince Albert died, Queen Victoria wore a black mourning dress for the remainder of her life. Today in Western culture, many people choose to wear black to funerals. However, other cultures express mourning through different colors: white in China and purple in Thailand.

28. Boutonnieres became popular in the early nineteenth century as lapel adornments. Paintings popularized this little buttonhole flower for men.

29. Lady Gaga keeps people guessing with her fashions: from super campy to sophisticated couture. The pop star always takes risks as she expresses her convention-defying style in unexpected ways.

30. After the children's novel *Little Lord Fauntleroy* was published in 1886, women dressed their young sons like the storybook character: velvet suits with lacy collars and long curls.

31. Natural beauty marks graced some famous faces, like that of actor Elizabeth Taylor. If people weren't born with these facial moles, they copied the French aristocracy, who wore faux beauty marks.

Medieval knights wore heavy chain mail into battle. Today, this body armor—coats, hoods, and gauntlets—can be spotted at Renaissance festivals around the country.

NASA developed 3-D printed metallic "space fabric" that resembles chain mail. The foldable fabric can change shape and both reflect and absorb light. Someday it could be used to protect astronauts and shield spacecraft from meteorites.

The magical slippers that Dorothy wears in Frank Baum's novel *The Wonderful Wizard of Oz* are silver, but the color was changed to ruby red in the 1939 film *The Wizard of Oz* because it popped out better against the yellow brick road.

Back when fabric was dyed primarily with natural substances, the Phoenicians created Tyrian purple using snotty snail mucus. Since this rare dye was so labor intensive, it was reserved for royalty. Royal purple dye was worth more than its weight in gold.

Queen Elizabeth I wore a mixture of lead and vinegar to whiten her face and cover her smallpox scars. While this concoction, known as Venetian ceruse, smoothed the queen's face, over time it caused hair loss, rotted teeth, and skin discoloration.

When Levi Strauss headed out to the California gold rush in 1853, he planned to sell tent canvas to prospectors. Instead, he ended up making durable blue jeans out of denim, which have been popular ever since.

Tie-dyed clothing is synonymous with colorful 1960s hippies, but this trend made a comeback during the pandemic. People stuck at home created their own splashy designs.

Fashions designed for people with visual impairments integrate braille into the clothes, allowing people to combine colors and dress themselves without assistance.

Adaptive clothing features stylish solutions for people with disabilities. Pants for wheelchair users have pull-up loops and no uncomfortable back pockets. Velcro and magnetic closures make it easy for people with physical challenges to get dressed. Other clothing has expanded openings and can be adjusted to fit prosthetics.

You now know 68 facts about PHENOMENAL FASHIONS!

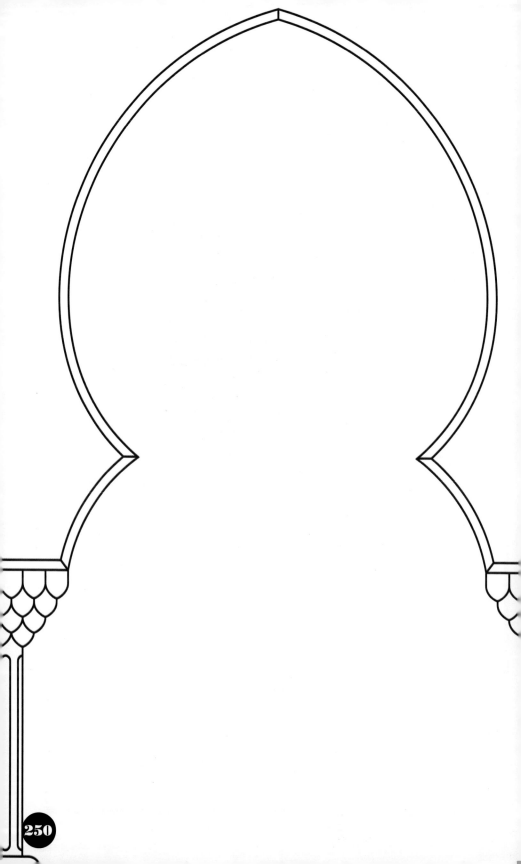

Outlandish History

If you thought history was full of boring facts found in dusty books, think again. These unexpected historical facts prove that history can be fascinating.

—

During the Middle Ages, barbers doubled as surgeons, cutting open veins and letting blood flow to treat every ailment from sore throat to plague. Today, barbers trim hair and give shaves, but their striped barbershop poles hint at their past: the red represents blood, the white represents bandages, and the pole stands for the stick patients squeezed to make their veins stand out.

Early dental technicians fashioned human teeth into dentures. Some of these teeth were sold by the desperately poor and others were robbed from graves. But looters pulled "Waterloo teeth" from the mouths of approximately forty-eight thousand soldiers killed in the 1815 battle.

The historic crossroads of Crown and John Streets in Kingston, New York, is known as America's oldest intersection. It's the only intersection where the buildings on all four corners were built before the Revolutionary War.

Boston's skinniest house is less than eleven feet wide. Built in 1884, the house is nicknamed Spite House due to sibling rivalry. Two brothers inherited the land; when one returned from the Civil War, he discovered his brother had constructed a massive home. He built his narrow house to block his brother's sunlight and views of the harbor.

Although the famous Leaning Tower of Pisa has a nearly four-degree lean thanks to an unstable foundation, it's not the farthest-leaning tower. That honor goes to the bell tower of the Church of Suurhusen in Germany, which leans at an angle of 5.1939 degrees.

The Anglo-Zanzibar War of 1896 was the shortest war in recorded history, lasting only forty minutes.

In the 1920s, way before GPS, people could wear a Plus Fours Routefinder on their wrist. Tiny maps rolled onto pegs could be scrolled via knobs to view the route and directions.

Back in the days before cheap, reliable alarm clocks, how did people wake up in time for work? A knocker-upper tapped on bedroom windows with a long wooden pole. (But who woke the knocker-upper up?)

Centuries ago, a naughty cat in Croatia walked across a medieval manuscript, leaving behind the evidence: inky paw prints.

The oldest known guard-dog sign dates back to the second century. The mosaic depicts a chained dog at the entrance to a villa in Pompeii. Below is the inscription *Cave Canem,* Latin for "Beware of the Dog."

In 1950, print advertisements for "A-Bomb Detergent" ran in newspapers. For $1, paranoid people could purchase liquid detergent in a soap-shaped container to scrub radioactive particles from their bodies.

The first customer service complaint ever recorded dates back thirty-eight hundred years ago. This Babylonian tablet logs a complaint about delivery of the wrong grade of copper.

Archeologists are still puzzling over the construction of Stonehenge. This circle of around one hundred massive upright stones was probably built in stages starting five thousand years ago. But how did primitive people move the stones—the largest weighs more than forty tons—and why?

In 1937, American aviator Amelia Earhart took off in an attempt to become the first pilot to circumnavigate the globe. She disappeared somewhere over the Pacific, and her Lockheed Electra L-10E plane was never found. This history mystery remains unsolved.

Louis II, known as Mad King Ludwig, went bankrupt building fairy-tale castles in the Bavarian mountains. His most famous, Neuschwanstein, inspired Disneyland's Sleeping Beauty Castle.

Candy saved the 1st Marine Division during the Korean War. Outnumbered and freezing when they met the enemy at Chosin Reservoir, the troops called in for more ammunition using the code name Tootsie Rolls. Imagine their surprise when crates of candy were airdropped instead of mortar shells! Tootsie Rolls gave the soldiers a sugar boost and, when chewed, acted as putty to plug bullet holes in equipment.

A Great Dane named Juliana became a World War II hero thanks to her remarkable bladder! The dog extinguished a bomb dropped by the Luftwaffe by peeing on it. Her quick thinking earned Juliana the 1941 Blue Cross medal.

The Voynich Manuscript continues to baffle scholars and scientists. No one has been able to decode the text, which is written in an unknown language. The parchment dates back to the early fifteenth century and also contains fantastical and colorful drawings.

British bureaucrats became alarmed about the number of venomous cobras infesting Delhi. They offered a bounty on cobra skins. However, this plan backfired when some Indians discovered a new cash crop: they bred snakes for their skins. When the British discovered this scam, they stopped paying the bounty. Cobra breeders turned their snakes loose and soon Delhi had an even worse infestation.

Something like the cobra problem happened when France occupied Vietnam. This time around, it was rats plaguing Hanoi. Officials offered a bounty on rodent tails, but once again citizens started breeding rats and cutting off their tails. After officials discovered this ruse, they stopped payments, and rats were released into the city.

Throughout history, people have invented gruesome torture devices that cause severe physical pain. These inventions were used as punishment or to extract information. Which of these is the most brutal?

1. Can someone be tortured by water? Absolutely—when cold water continuously drips onto prisoners' foreheads, it elicits confessions and eventually drives them insane. An Italian lawyer first described this water torture machine in the sixteenth century.

2. Waterboarding was first documented in the fourteenth century. There were two different forms of this interrogation. Water was either directly pumped into victims' stomachs, or their throats were filled with a steady stream of water until they drowned in slow motion.

3. The Spanish Inquisition was infamous for severe tortures. Some citizens condemned for their religious beliefs were lowered onto the sharp point of a Judas cradle. This tall pyramid-shaped device would slowly impale the victims.

4. Women accused of witchcraft might have their thumbs or other digits slowly crushed in the thumbscrew.

5. Executioners used the head crusher to extract confessions. They slowly turned the screw so that a metal cap lowered and compressed the victim's head until the brain was squashed.

6. The Iron Maiden was a seven-foot-tall sarcophagus with an interior studded with spikes. Once victims were shut inside, the spikes would pierce the chest, back, and eyes. It could take days before the victim finally died.

7. Prisoners were locked inside a hollow chamber within a torture device called the brazen bull. The executioner lit a fire underneath this huge bronze bull, and the unfortunate victims roasted to death, their screams amplified through pipes so they sounded like a bull bellowing.

8. Victims stretched on the rack—a rectangular frame with rollers at either end—would have every bone in their body dislocated and their limbs torn out. Prisoners waiting their turn in this torture device would often confess on the spot.

9. Starting in 1792, the guillotine was used in France to execute thousands of people. A razor-sharp blade would forcefully sever the victim's head from the body. The last decapitation in France occurred in 1977.

10. Crocodile shears awaited those who attempted to assassinate the king. The insides of these cutting tools resembled a reptile's mouth with rows of spikes. When heated, the shears were clamped down on the would-be assassinators' appendages.

Many civilizations preserved the bodies of their dead through mummification. Mummies continue to reveal secrets, even though they've been dead for thousands of years.

1. Ancient Egyptians were famous for their elaborate mummies. They believed that the body needed to be preserved in a lifelike form in order to live again after death.

2. It took around seventy days to create a mummy. Special priests with a knowledge of anatomy worked as embalmers. They removed the organs and placed them in special canopic jars.

3. Embalmers left only the heart in the body. This organ was considered the core of a person and the center of intelligence, rather than the brain. Egyptians believed the heart would be weighed in the afterlife to reveal if the person had led a good life.

4. Priests removed the brain by inserting a curved metal tool through the nostrils. Since it was believed to be useless, the brain was discarded.

5. Then the body and organs were packed in salt to remove all moisture. Egypt's arid climate helped speed up this process.

6. The dried-out body was washed and wrapped in hundreds of yards of linen. Resin helped these strips of linen to stick to the body.

7. To protect the dead on his or her trip through the afterlife, priests wrote magical words on some of the bandages. They also wrapped amulets—lucky charms—within the linen.

8. Meanwhile, workers prepared the burial chamber, filling it with everything necessary for the afterlife: paintings, food, clothing, weapons, jewelry, furniture, boats, and chariots.

9. Some ancient Egyptian pharaohs were accompanied to the afterlife with servants and pets.

10. Finally, the mummified body was placed in a sarcophagus, an elaborate coffin that resembled a human, and sealed up inside the burial chamber.

11. Egyptians also mummified animals, whom they viewed as incarnations of the gods. They sacrificed many sacred animals including cats, crocodiles, ibis, cobras, bulls, and baboons.

12. Perhaps the most famous Egyptian tomb was that of King Tutankhamun, the boy pharaoh who died at around age nineteen. After mummification, a solid gold burial mask weighing twenty-four pounds—decorated with a coiled serpent and false beard–was placed over his head. Then King Tut was placed in three nestled golden coffins that were fitted into his granite sarcophagus.

13. More than five thousand artifacts and treasures were crammed into King Tut's tomb. They included a board game called Senet, a statue of the jackal god of death Anubis, perfume vessels, chariots and thrones, and 130 walking sticks.

14. What killed King Tut? When scientists extracted samples from his mummy, they found evidence of malaria and a crippling bone disorder in his clubbed left foot. Many theories still swirl around, including the latest: the boy king died from an infection caused by a broken leg.

15. Inbreeding also likely contributed to King Tut's poor health. DNA tests revealed that the boy king's parents were brother and sister. King Tut was married to his half sister, Queen Ankhesenamun.

16. Not all mummies were planned—some happened by accident. More than one hundred mummies discovered in aboveground crypts in Guanajuato, Mexico, had been interred during a cholera outbreak in 1833 to stop the spread of disease. Instead of decaying, the dead were accidentally mummified through extreme heat and minerals in the soil.

17. When relatives of the dead didn't pay a local tax, the accidental mummies of Guanajuato were disinterred and stored in a building. Cemetery workers charged tourists a few pesos for a torchlight viewing. Today, modern-day visitors can tour the Museo de las Momias, or Mummy Museum.

18. Buddhist monks from the Shingon sect in Japan practiced a DIY form of mummification . . . while still alive! They ate an extreme diet, foraging on foods found in the forest that promoted decay, like nuts and roots. Once body fat and muscle disappeared, the monks drank a special tea so their bodies were inhospitable to corpse-eating insects.

19. Disciples buried the monks alive in a pine box. They inserted a bamboo tube through the lid. As the monk meditated in his tomb, he rang a bell to signal that he was still alive. When the ringing stopped and the disciples confirmed that the monk had died, they sealed the tomb.

20. After one thousand days underground, the monk was unearthed. His disciples inspected him for decay. If the body stayed intact, the monk had achieved his goal: becoming "a Buddha in this body." His mummy would then be enshrined in a temple.

21. Mummy medicine? Between the twelfth and seventeenth centuries, apothecaries used ground-up mummies as health food. They sold the powder to cure everything from headaches to tumors.

22. In 2021, Egyptians threw a parade for royalty. But the guests of honor were twenty-two queens and kings who had died more than three thousand years ago. Carriages transported the mummies to their new resting place: the National Museum of Egyptian Civilization.

US presidents have received some strange gifts throughout history. Which of these would you accept and which would you decline?

1. Dairy farmers in New York gifted Andrew Jackson a mammoth wheel of cheese that arrived at the White House in a cart pulled by twenty-four horses. The cheese ripened in the foyer for two years before Jackson invited the public to sample it. Two hours later, the only thing that remained was the smell.

2. In 1862, Abraham Lincoln wrote a polite letter to the king of Siam declining his offer of live elephants. Steam power, Lincoln pointed out, had overtaken the need for animal power.

3. George Washington wanted a certain breed of male donkey found only in Spain. He planned to crossbreed this animal with his female horses to produce a strong hybrid: the mule. After many attempts, Washington finally got his donkey, whom he named Royal Gift, from the king of Spain.

4. Thomas Jefferson declined presents from foreign dignitaries, but he made an exception when the Tunisian ambassador gifted the president with four Arabian horses. The sale of the horses, Jefferson reasoned, would pay for the cost of the ambassador's visit to Washington, DC.

5. During a dinner in Beijing, first lady Patricia Nixon remarked how much she liked giant pandas. The Chinese premier sent Ling-Ling and Hsing-Hsing as a gift to Patricia and Richard Nixon. The giant pandas resided at the National Zoo, where they attracted millions of fans from around the world.

6. Harry S. Truman received an early birthday present from his fellow Missourians: a bowling alley. The president hadn't bowled since he was a teenager, but he encouraged his staff to form the White House Bowling League.

7. When Soviet leader Nikita Khrushchev sent John F. Kennedy a puppy named Pushinka, it was like he was thumbing his nose at the president. Pushinka's mother was Strelka, a dog the Soviets had sent on a trip aboard Sputnik 5 to orbit Earth. This had put Moscow ahead in the space race, but Kennedy vowed to put a person on the moon by the end of the 1960s.

8. Queen Victoria gifted Rutherford B. Hayes with a desk made from the oak timbers of the British ship HMS *Resolute*. After the ship became locked in ice in the Arctic, it was abandoned but later found by an American whaling ship and returned to the queen. Decades later, she had the Resolute desk built as a thank-you gift.

In 1916, Jeannette Rankin became the first woman in history elected to the US House of Representatives. American women weren't guaranteed the right to vote until the 19th Amendment was ratified in 1920.

Women were banned from running in the Boston Marathon until 1972. However, in 1966, Roberta Gibb ran the race after receiving a letter that stated, "Women aren't allowed, and furthermore are not physiologically able." Gibb hid in bushes, then slipped into the pack, and finished in the top third.

The copyright to the lyrics of one of the world's most popular songs, "Happy Birthday to You," was ruled invalid in 2015. Now the song, written in the 1890s, will no longer earn $2 million in annual royalties and is finally free to sing.

The Olympics held art competitions from 1912 to 1948. Winners received gold, silver, and bronze medals for architecture, art, literature, and music. Since it was difficult to determine the amateur status of the artists, the Olympics stopped the art competitions.

Vessels passing through the Panama Canal pay fees ranging from around $2,000 for small yachts on up to nearly $1 million for container ships. However, the lowest toll was only 36 cents, paid in 1928 when a swimmer passed through.

The world's smallest country, Vatican City, occupies less than one square mile and has a population of about 900 people. But thanks to pickpockets and other petty criminals preying on millions of tourists, the Vatican has one of the highest crime rates in the world.

New York City's Empire State Building was the world's first building with more than one hundred stories. Today, it's the most photographed building on Earth. This city within a city even has its own zip code: 10118.

The Eiffel Tower was originally intended for Barcelona, but the Spanish city rejected Gustave Eiffel's plans, believing the tower would be an eyesore. Today this landmark towers over the city of Paris, where it welcomes more than seven million visitors each year.

Con man Victor Lustig "sold" the Eiffel Tower for scrap metal to the highest bidder. Amazingly, he pulled off this scam twice!

Pink is the color of shame for Thai police officers who step out of line by littering or showing up late to work. They're forced to wear something embarrassing: a pink Hello Kitty armband!

In 1934, the US Treasury printed $100,000 bills with Woodrow Wilson's portrait on them. The bills never circulated among the general public.

Today, the largest US currency in circulation is the $100 bill. In 1969, the treasury discontinued $500, $1,000, $5,000, and $10,000 notes due to lack of use.

The 1928 movie *Woman in the Moon* was the first to use the "3-2-1" countdown. Fritz Lang's silent film inspired NASA to use countdowns before rocket launches.

Even a $10 million reward didn't solve the mystery of the world's largest property theft. Thirteen artworks valued at $500 million were stolen from Boston's Isabella Stewart Gardner Museum in 1990. Two thieves dressed as police officers stole the masterpieces in a scant eighty-one minutes.

You now know 74 facts about OUTLANDISH HISTORY!

Curious Inventions

From Stone Age tools to the latest electronics, humans have been creating objects that never existed before. Maybe one of these inventions will inspire you to create your own unique product.

—

Who doesn't love toys and games? The stories behind their inventions are almost as much fun as these playthings!

1. G.I. Joe was pitched to Hasbro as "a military themed, Barbie-inspired toy line." The toy company coined the term "action figure" in 1964 to market these toys to boys.

2. Ancient versions of G.I. Joe were crafted from clay and modeled on Roman gladiators.

3. While the National Toy Hall of Fame named the humble stick as the world's oldest toy, other playthings were handmade. One of the oldest was a four-thousand-year-old stone doll unearthed on a Mediterranean island along with miniature terra-cotta cooking pots.

4. An ancient ceramic baby rattle found in Turkey is also four thousand years old.

5. Invented in ancient China, the yo-yo was originally used as a weapon.

6. A London engraver created the first jigsaw puzzle in 1767, not to entertain but to educate. Teachers used his puzzle—a map of the world—to teach students geography.

7. Alphabet blocks first appeared in 1693. Later, Friedrich Froebel observed children playing in his kindergarten, which he pioneered in 1837, and created educational play materials including geometric wooden shapes.

8. The German toy company Steiff designed a teddy bear with jointed arms and legs in 1902. The mohair bear was modeled after real bears sketched at the zoo.

9. Also in 1902, a Brooklyn, New York, shopkeeper and his wife made a stuffed fabric bear and displayed it in their window with a sign: Teddy's bear. This bear was inspired by President Theodore "Teddy" Roosevelt's refusal to shoot a bear during a hunting trip. The couple started a successful toy company to manufacture teddy bears.

10. A Scottish scientist invented a tube filled with loose pieces of colored glass that were reflected by mirrors to create patterns. He called his 1816 invention the kaleidoscope, Greek for "beautiful form watcher."

11. Invented in 1896, the USA Liquid Pistol used water as ammo to stop dangerous dogs and humans "without permanent injury."

12. Twenty years after the liquid water pistol, the Cachoo Sneeze Powder Company released its water-streaming lapel flower.

13. The practical joke company got its start in 1904 selling sneezing powder; the FDA banned Cachoo in the early 1940s.

14. The Cachoo Sneeze Powder Company was renamed S.S. Adams after its founder, who went on to invent more than six hundred novelty-based gags, magic tricks, and puzzles. One of its most iconic is the Joy Buzzer, patented in 1932 and used by practical jokers to vibrate when pressed into unsuspecting victims' palms.

15. A NASA engineer invented the Power Drencher in 1989. Renamed the Super Soaker, it triggered the water-blaster craze.

16. After accidentally knocking coiled wires off a shelf, a mechanical engineer watched in amazement as they tumbled across the floor. Soon millions of people wanted one of his Slinky toys.

17. When the NERF ball was introduced in 1969, it was advertised as the world's first indoor ball that wouldn't hurt babies or elderly people.

18. While recovering from polio in a hospital, a retired schoolteacher invented Candy Land to help distract other children in the polio ward. The board game continues to sell around one million units each year.

19. LEGO patented its famous colorful interlocking bricks in 1958. Its name is a Danish abbreviation for "play well."

20. How many ways can six of the standard eight-studded LEGO bricks be combined? The astonishing answer: 915,103,765 ways!

21. Video games were launched in scientists' research labs. One of the first created in 1952 (as a PhD thesis) was called OXO, or tic-tac-toe.

22. Game Boy, the first portable handheld game system, debuted in 1989. Its Japanese manufacturer, Nintendo, started off in 1889 making playing cards.

23. Designers at a toy company took apart a tricycle and jumbled up the parts, creating Big Wheel, a low-riding plastic trike that ruled the road.

24. A company that manufactured red barn paint listened to teachers' requests for safe, affordable wax sticks. Then the company created multicolored crayons and came up with a name based on the French words for "chalk" and "oily": Crayola.

25. The first boxes containing eight Crayola crayons rolled off the assembly line in 1903. They sold for a nickel.

26. A putty designed to clean coal soot off of wallpaper found a more popular use as a modeling compound for kids: Play-Doh.

27. Colorful plastic hula-hoops became a fad in the 1950s. However, children have been playing with hoops made out of metal, wood, and dried willow for thousands of years.

28. Architect Frank Lloyd Wright's son, John, followed in his father's footsteps as the inventor of Lincoln Logs, a log-based construction toy.

29. When Mr. Potato Head debuted in 1952, the kit contained only plastic eyes, ears, noses, and mouths. Kids had to supply their own potatoes! Later a plastic potato body was included.

30. The plastic spud made history that year as the first children's toy to be advertised on television. Mr. Potato Head ushered in the age of "pester power," with children nagging their parents for products spotlighted in TV commercials.

31. People handmade ancient marbles out of pebbles, bones, clay, and marble stone. Later, glassblowers created colored glass marbles. When the first marble factory opened in the early 1900s, a special machine mass-produced ten thousand marbles per day.

32. A French electrician invented a mechanical drawing tablet that he named the Magic Screen. Renamed Etch A Sketch by the Ohio Art Company, the toy became popular with doodlers of all ages.

33. When the Etch A Sketch was featured in *Toy Story* and *Toy Story 2*, its appearance lifted sales out of a slump. This toy went on to sell more than one hundred million units worldwide.

34. Ernő Rubik, a Hungarian professor, invented his colorful puzzle toy to teach his students about 3-D geometry. Rubik's Cube has 43,252,003,274,489,856,000 possible combinations, but only one solution.

35. The world's record for solving the Rubik's Cube is 3.47 seconds—for a human that is. A robot solved the cube in an incredible 0.38 seconds!

36. The inspiration behind Raggedy Ann came from a beat-up doll that a girl discovered in her grandmother's attic. The girl's father, illustrator Johnny Gruelle, secured a patent for the doll in 1915, but sadly his daughter died. Her father carried on in her memory, and today Raggedy Ann still has her signature "I love you" embroidered on her heart.

37. The Barbie doll's creator, Ruth Handler, thought there might be a market for a doll that wasn't based on an infant. She modeled Barbie on a German fashion doll called Bild Lilli.

38. More than a billion Barbie dolls have been sold since they first made their appearance in 1959. That averages out to about three sold every second in more than 150 countries.

39. Barbie's first pet was a pony, and more than forty other pets followed, including dogs, cats, horses, a parrot, and exotics: the chimpanzee, giraffe, lion cub, panda, and zebra.

40. When toy manufacturer Mattel released a talking Barbie that said "Math is hard," feminists banded together to combat gender stereotypes in toys. Some switched the voice boxes on hundreds of Barbie dolls with G.I. Joe action figures before replacing them on toy store shelves.

Toilet paper has been around since the sixth century, but more modern inventions led to its widespread use. Gayetty's Medicated Paper, the first commercially packaged toilet paper, was sold in flat sheets starting in 1857.

The Scott Paper Company put toilet paper on rolls in 1890.

In 1897, Albany Perforated Wrapping Paper sold perforated toilet paper. This would lead to an ongoing debate: should the toilet paper be hung over or under the roll? According to the diagram for the original patent, Team Over is the winner!

The first commercially produced mouthwash, Odol, hit the market in 1892; it's still available today. Way back in 1 CE, ancient Romans swished their mouths with bottled urine—a practice that continued until the eighteenth century.

When Marvin Stone realized that the rye grass and reeds that people used to sip liquids were growing musty, he invented the first paper drinking straws.

Inventing is a risky business.
Many products fail, but they inspire inventors to take risks and try, try again. Some of the world's most notorious flops are showcased in Sweden's Museum of Failure.

1. Sometimes a colossal failure evolves into a success. The Apple Newton, a "personal digital assistant," failed to live up to expectations. However, it eventually led to the phenomenally successful iPad.

2. Green ketchup anyone? The Heinz EZ Squirt became an instant hit with kids, but sales of this food fad fizzled out.

3. There were high expectations when the Ford Edsel launched in 1957. But this medium-priced car hit the market at the wrong time: people wanted compact cars.

4. Rejuvenique promised to tone facial muscles using electricity. This creepy-looking beauty mask was never FDA-approved—plus users likened the pain to a thousand ants biting their face!

5. When consumers picked Pepsi over Coca-Cola in blind taste tests, Coca-Cola changed its classic recipe and launched New Coke. Coke die-hards nixed the sweeter product, and after only seventy-seven days, the original formula was brought back.

6. The futuristic DeLorean car looked cool with its gull-wing doors, plus it starred as a time machine in the movie *Back to the Future.* However, this expensive sports car had a major flaw: it lacked power.

7. The food additive olestra sounded promising . . . on paper. Olestra removed unwanted fat when added to snack foods such as potato chips, but caused extremely unpleasant side effects.

A spectacle maker from the Netherlands, Hans Lippershey, changed the course of astronomy in 1608: he invented the first telescope.

One year later, in 1609, Italian astronomer Galileo promptly made a series of increasingly powerful telescopes.

Naturalist Charles Darwin created the wheeled office chair in the 1840s. He attached wheels to his armchair so he could glide around his workspace and easily reach his specimens.

The Volkswagen, or "people's car," was the brain-child of two designers in Nazi Germany: Ferdinand Porsche and Adolf Hitler. In 1934, Hitler instructed Porsche to create a car that could be mass-produced for Germany's new road network.

The small, affordable Volkswagen Beetle became the world's most popular car; more than 21.5 million were sold between 1945 and 2003.

Two Greek architects invented a house that's built into a cliff overlooking the Aegean Sea. The house, named Casa Brutale, uses heavy forms and industrial materials and is topped with a massive swimming pool that brings in natural light and provides insulation.

Elis Stenman designed machines that made paper clips, but he didn't stop there. The mechanical engineer built his summer home out of paper and created all the furniture using logs of paper.

The first candy canes were all white. In 1670, a choirmaster at a German cathedral bent sugar sticks into the shape of canes, similar to a shepherd's staff. These treats were used to pacify children during long church services.

When James Naismith, a Canadian sports coach, took a soccer ball and a peach basket to the YMCA gym in 1891, he invented a new sport: basketball!

College students tossed empty pie tins from the Frisbie Pie Company; throwers would yell "Frisbie" to signal the catcher. The flying disc game soared to new heights when an inventor designed a molded plastic disc in 1948: the Flying-Saucer.

A Greek mathematician invented the first robot—a steam-powered flying dove—in 350 BCE. This robotic bird could flap its wings and fly more than 650 feet.

During the eighteenth century, a French inventor created life-size robots that played musical instruments, like the flute and tambourine. But the inventor became famous for his robotic duck, which imitated the motions of a live duck—and could quack, drink, eat, and poop!

Johns Hopkins engineers chased cockroaches through an obstacle course to study how they moved across rough terrain. Then they invented search-and-rescue robots that imitated the roaches' jittery movements: pushing, climbing, running, and diving.

Spot, a famous robot dog designed by Boston Dynamics, has a new mission: two of the $75,000 robotic canines are being used by the New York Fire Department to aid firefighters in search and rescue missions. Dalmatians, step aside!

Swiss scientists invented Cheetah-cub, a robot that moves like a cat using springs and small motors. Speedy and lightweight, the catlike robot is designed to be used in exploration and search-and-rescue missions.

Instead of flies, a robot made with severed pieces of a Venus flytrap grabs delicate objects, like thin wire.

Engineers at a university in Peru are pulling clean water out of humid air. They invented a water-collecting billboard that generates about ninety-six liters of water each day. The billboard is installed in Lima; it is one of the driest places on Earth, with almost no rainfall but high humidity.

Vending machines have a long history. If you think they just sell junk food, sugary drinks, gum, and lottery tickets, check out all these unusual items offered via automated retailing machines.

1. An ancient Greek mathematician invented the first vending machine to dispense holy water.

2. The first coin-operated vending machine appeared in London railway stations in the early 1880s. It sold stamps and postcards.

3. When Thomas Adams invented a fruit-flavored gum called Tutti-Frutti, he made machines to sell his gum at New York City subway stations. Starting in 1888, riders could buy a piece of gum for one penny.

4. Starting in 1902, the Horn & Hardart automat served fresh hot meals. All of the food came out of vending machines. Hungry customers peered into glass door compartments to choose their dishes; then they dropped coins into a slot, turned a knob to open the door, and removed their food. Horn & Hardart quickly became the largest restaurant chain in the world, serving eight hundred thousand meals per day.

5. Modern vending machines offer surprising things. You can buy organic raw milk, fruits and vegetables, baguettes, sneakers, and even gold to-go at a hotel in the United Arab Emirates.

6. An unusual vending machine in Turkey recycles plastic bottles and in exchange dispenses water and dog food.

7. In 2016, an opulent vending machine at Autobahn Motors in Singapore sold luxury cars: Ferraris and Lamborghinis.

8. Students in some elementary schools receive gold coins designed for vending machines that dispense books.

9. Japan is the vending machine capital of the world, with one vending machine for every thirty people. Junk food is rarely dispensed. Instead, customers insert money to obtain a bottle of broth with an entire grilled fish, fresh bananas, and rhino beetle treats.

**You now know 77 facts about
CURIOUS INVENTIONS!**

Fantastic Dinosaurs

The first dinosaurs appeared around 245 million years ago. They spread to every continent. Take an armchair trip back to the age of dinosaurs.

—

Dinosaurs displayed an amazing amount of different shapes and sizes. Some were as small as a chicken and weighed eight pounds. Others stretched more than 120 feet long and weighed eighty tons.

Dinosaurs lived during the Mesozoic era, which is divided into three periods: Triassic (252–201 million years ago), Jurassic (201–145 million years ago), and Cretaceous (145–66 million years ago).

Dinosaurs slowly developed from giant reptiles that lived on Earth more than 280 million years ago. Today's reptiles are distant cousins of dinosaurs.

Dinosaurs have a hole in the hip socket, a feature that distinguishes them from other reptiles. This allowed dinosaurs to walk upright.

A Victorian scientist invented the word *dinosaur* in 1842. The word means "terrible lizard."

The first dinosaur to be named was *Megalosaurus* in 1824. Its name means "great fossil lizard."

Chinese paleontologists gave a tiny dinosaur the longest genus name: *Pachycephalosaurus,* which means "tiny thick-headed lizard."

Paleontologists, scientists who study the fossils of animals and plants that lived very long ago, estimate that around seven hundred species of dinosaurs have been discovered and named.

All dinosaurs hatched from eggs, ranging from tiny to volleyball-size. Some dinosaurs brooded, or sat on top of their eggs to incubate them.

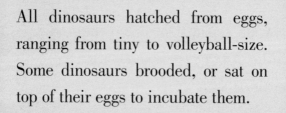

Researchers studied growth lines on fossils of dinosaur embryos to determine how long it took eggs to hatch. Incubation ranged from three to six months depending on the dinosaur.

Not all dinosaur eggs were hard-shelled like modern-day birds' eggs. Some laid soft, leathery eggs similar to those of today's turtles.

Hefty dinosaurs could not sit on their soft-shelled eggs to hatch them. Instead, they probably buried the eggs in sand or moist soil and covered them with plants to incubate.

Some dinosaurs laid colored eggs, including spotted and speckled. Before paleontologists analyzed dinosaur eggshell samples from around the world, they believed that only birds had colored eggs.

Discoveries of fossilized dinosaur eggs are rare, and rarer still are embryos found inside those eggs. However, in 1993, scientists discovered an embryo of an *Oviraptorid* that dated 80 million years ago.

Paleontologists digging in Montana found a nesting colony they called Egg Mountain. This mass grave contained fossils of duck-billed dinosaurs from eighty million years ago: eggs, hatchlings, juveniles, and adults.

These duck-billed dinosaurs were named *Maiasaura,* which is Greek for "caring mother lizard."

In 1985, a group of middle-school students helped crown the *Maiasaura* as Montana's state fossil.

In 2019, a ten-year-old boy in China discovered a nesting site containing eleven dinosaur eggs. The dinosaur egg fossils date back to sixty-six million years ago.

The eleven dinosaur eggs joined the collection at Heyuan Dinosaur Museum in China. The museum has more than ten thousand dinosaur eggs—the world's largest collection.

Even though *Albertosaurus* was smaller than its Tyrannosaurus rex (also known as T. Rex) cousin, this fierce predator was at the top of its food chain. It had serrated teeth shaped like bananas and hunted in packs.

**Which dinosaur inspires
equal doses of awe and terror?
If you guessed *T. rex*, you're correct.**

1. *Tyrannosaurus rex* can be translated into "king of the tyrant lizards."

2. Weighing up to nine tons, *T. rex* was one of the largest predators to live on Earth. This dinosaur underwent a growth spurt as a teenager, gaining up to 3,950 pounds per year.

3. This tyrant lizard was almost as tall as a giraffe and heavier than an elephant.

4. Everything about *T. rex* was huge, except for its arms! Although powerfully muscled, the dinosaur's arms were too short to grab prey or reach its mouth.

5. *T. rex*'s huge mouth contained around sixty teeth with jagged edges. They could crush skulls, pelvises, and bones of other dinosaurs.

6. And *T. rex* could replace worn-out or lost teeth, but this process could take up to two years.

7. *T. rex* had the strongest bite of any land animal to ever live.

8. As you'd expect from such a massive dinosaur, *T. rex* had humongous poop that weighed 20.5 pounds— around as much as a six-month-old baby!

9. The best-preserved *T. rex* ever discovered is on display at Chicago's Field Museum. This dinosaur is nicknamed Sue after Sue Hendrickson, who discovered the fossil in South Dakota.

10. Sue is the largest *T. rex* ever unearthed. She stands twelve feet high and stretches forty-two feet long.

11. The Native American rancher who owned the property where Sue was found sold the fossil at auction. Within eight minutes, the Field Museum purchased Sue for $8.36 million.

12. That record was smashed when *T. rex* Stan sold for $31.8 million.

In 2019, a new species of dinosaur was discovered in England on the Isle of Wight. Scientists named the dinosaur *Vectaerovenator* and determined that it's related to *T. rex.*

Paleontologists believe that *Argentinosaurus,* discovered in Argentina in 1993, could be the record holder as the world's largest dinosaur. It measured up to 130 feet long and weighed up to 110 tons.

Herds of *Argentinosaurus* plodded around the plains and forests of South America, eating up to 220 pounds of plants daily.

Another new species was excavated in Argentina's Patagonia region in 2014. Measuring 122 feet long, *Patagotitan mayorum* was displayed by the American Museum of Natural History—with its head and neck extending out toward the elevator banks.

Scientists named another *supermassive* dinosaur discovered in Patagonia after a steel warship: *Dreadnoughtus*. They estimated that it weighed sixty tons, stood two stories high at its shoulder, and measured eighty-five feet long.

Estimating the weight and length of dinosaurs is difficult when only partial skeletons remain. Some paleontologists compare the bones in living animals, such as an elephant, with those of a dinosaur. Others use 3-D reconstructions to get an idea of what the dinosaur looked like while alive.

Ornithopods were a group of gentle herbivores that stood on two legs. In fact, their name means "bird foot."

Paleontologists estimate that *Ornithomimus* could run at speeds of up to forty miles per hour. Jamaican sprinter Usain Bolt, the world's fastest person, can "only" attain a top speed of 27.33 miles per hour.

Just how do paleontologists determine the speed of dinosaurs? They study sequences of footprints, called trackways, preserved as fossils. Then they use equations based on the distance between footfalls and physical factors, such as the size and shape of the dinosaur's legs and feet.

Paleontologists can discover the age of dinosaurs by counting annual growth rings in fossil thighbones. This method is similar to counting tree rings.

A South African dinosaur's growth rate corresponded to environmental factors such as climate and diet. *Massospondylus* might have doubled in size if there was lots of rain and plants to eat. But if food was scarce, growth of this dinosaur might have been cut back.

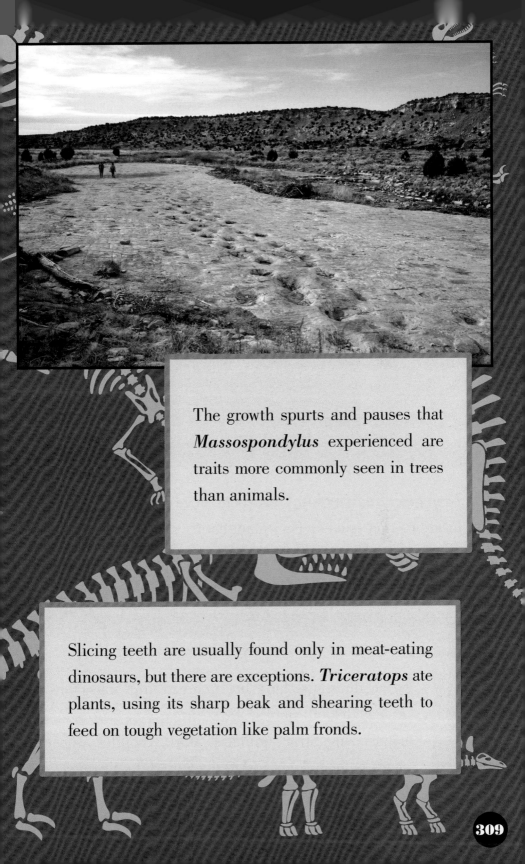

The growth spurts and pauses that *Massospondylus* experienced are traits more commonly seen in trees than animals.

Slicing teeth are usually found only in meat-eating dinosaurs, but there are exceptions. *Triceratops* ate plants, using its sharp beak and shearing teeth to feed on tough vegetation like palm fronds.

Hadrosaurs had up to 960 teeth designed for chopping and grinding up plants. One of these duck-billed dinosaurs discovered in Wyoming had fossil plant remains in its stomach, which scientists identified as pine needles.

Dracorex hogwartsia had a bony head covered in knobs and spikes. This plant-eating dinosaur was named the "dragon king of Hogwarts" after the academy for wizards in the Harry Potter series.

Other dinosaurs have been named after musicians. A snaggletooth named *Masiakasaurus knopfleri* honors Dire Straits guitarist Mark Knopfler, whose songs paleontologists were playing while digging.

Stegosaurus means "roofed lizard," a reference to the plates staggered along on its back. Paleontologists have different theories about the function of these plates. Some believe that *Stegosaurus* used its bony plates and the three-foot-long spikes on its tail as defense against predators.

Blood vessels near the surface of *Stegosaurus*'s plates could absorb heat from the sun and help the dinosaur warm up.

Although *Stegosaurus* was around the size of a school bus, it had a tiny brain about as small as a walnut.

Farmers in China discovered *Sinosauropteryx*. Its name means "first Chinese dragon feather," referring to the hairlike feathers covering its body.

Sinosauropteryx was also the first dinosaur to have its color—a gingery orange—confirmed by scientists using an electron microscope. This dinosaur had ginger and white stripes on its tail.

Despite its twelve-inch talons, *Nothronychus* wasn't a meat eater. This vegetarian had a huge potbelly that helped it digest all the plants it ate. Its name means "slothlike claw."

A down coat of shaggy feathers covered *Nothronychus*. This plant eater resembled a modern-day emu.

The fierce *Deinonychus* was also covered with feathers. It used five-inch-long sickle-shaped talons to pin down prey and seventy bladelike teeth to rip flesh and crunch bones.

The massive *Triceratops* was named after its three-horned face. This slow-moving plant eater used its horns for defense. These spikes could grow up to three feet, as long as a toddler.

Triceratops's huge head made up a third of its length—a maximum of thirty feet—and was surrounded by an impressive neck frill that it used to attract females.

Paleontologists in Mexico identified a new species of dinosaur in 2021. They named the crested dinosaur *Tlatolophus galorum*.

The crest of *Tlatolophus galorum* could have been a bright color such as red, or multicolored with spots. Scientists believe that this dinosaur saw its world in color, like modern-day birds.

And, like today's elephants, *Tlatolophus galorum* used low-frequency sounds to communicate.

Another newly described dinosaur, *Menefeeceratops,* had a horned head and frills, along with a beaked face. It lived in New Mexico eighty-two million years ago.

A chicken-size dinosaur, *Shuvuuia,* had amazing hearing and night vision, similar to today's barn owl. Scientists believe this dinosaur hunted small prey in complete darkness.

Shuvuuia lived in the deserts of Mongolia. Its skeleton had a strange combination of features: a birdlike skull, muscular arms with one claw on each hand, and long legs like a roadrunner.

The discovery of a tiny birdlike skull preserved in amber is helping scientists understand the evolution of birds. This miniature dinosaur was even smaller than the tiniest bird alive today: the bee hummingbird.

But unlike the bee hummingbird, this mini dinosaur had jaws packed with more than one hundred teeth.

Four-legged plant eaters, *Ankylosaurs* were heavily armored with bones that grew in the skin. Rows of spikes on their flanks, bony knobs on their backs, and a long tail tipped with a bony sledgehammer-like feature acted as a defense against predators.

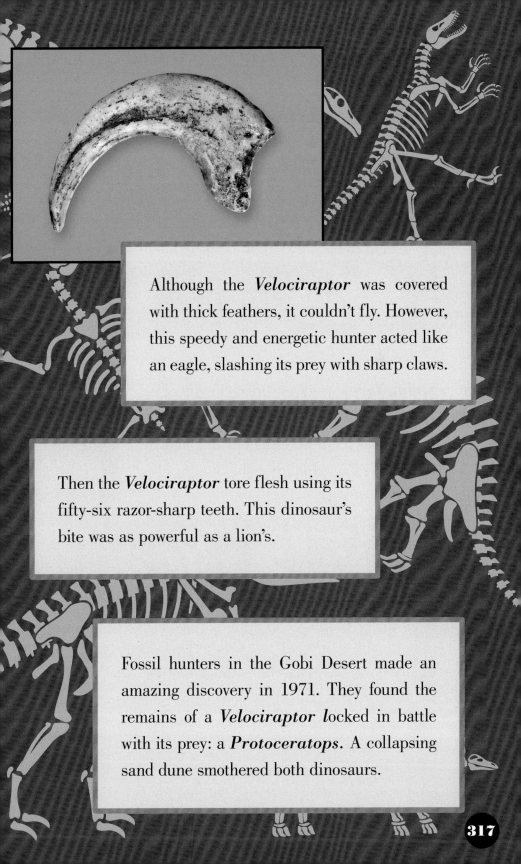

Although the *Velociraptor* was covered with thick feathers, it couldn't fly. However, this speedy and energetic hunter acted like an eagle, slashing its prey with sharp claws.

Then the *Velociraptor* tore flesh using its fifty-six razor-sharp teeth. This dinosaur's bite was as powerful as a lion's.

Fossil hunters in the Gobi Desert made an amazing discovery in 1971. They found the remains of a *Velociraptor* locked in battle with its prey: a *Protoceratops*. A collapsing sand dune smothered both dinosaurs.

Baryonyx was a predator, but instead of hunting on land, this dinosaur ruled the water. It snatched fish from the water using long jaws similar to those of a crocodile and ninety-six sharp teeth. *Baryonyx* also used long claws on its thumbs like a spear.

Spinosaurus used sensors on the tip of its snout to hunt fish. Instead of curved and serrated, its teeth were smooth and conical so it could snag slippery fish.

Spinosaurus, or "spined reptile," was named for the gigantic sail on its back. Scientists believe that the dinosaur used its sail to attract mates.

Giraffatitan means "giant giraffe," and this dinosaur rose as tall as a five-story building to graze on treetops. It was around seventy-five feet long, with its neck making up around half of its length.

When scientists first discovered *Giraffatitan*, nostrils perched on top of its head baffled them. At first, they thought this sauropod lived in water, using water to support its weight and its long neck and high nostrils as a type of snorkel!

A dinosaur the size of a guinea pig could glide between trees. *Microraptor* used large claws on its feet to climb trees, feathers on its legs to help it steer, and long feathers on its arms to help it glide like a flying squirrel.

A birdlike dinosaur as tall as *T. rex* was thirty-five times larger than its closest relation. The scientist who discovered *Gigantoraptor* in China described his find as "like having a mouse that is the size of a horse or cow."

Antarctic dinosaurs are surrounded in mystery since fossil hunting is difficult on this frozen continent. But back in the age of dinosaurs, Antarctica was covered in forests. One celebrated dinosaur discovered in 1991, *Cryolophosaurus,* is nicknamed Elvisaurus for its bizarre headgear—a forward-facing curved crest that resembles a pompadour!

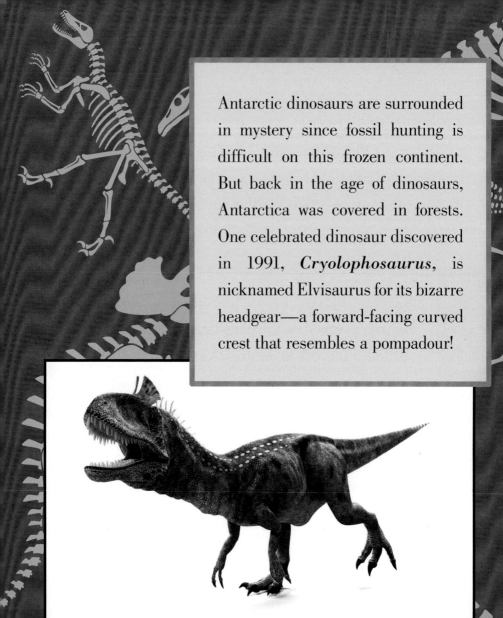

Dinosaurs vanished about sixty-five million years ago when a huge meteorite crashed into Earth. The six-mile-wide rock from outer space smashed into what is now the Yucatán Peninsula in Mexico.

The meteorite impact ignited huge fires, and clouds of dust blocked out the sun, killing plants. Then plant-eating dinosaurs starved, followed by meat eaters.

Not all animals perished in this mass extinction. Birds survived. Today, many scientists believe that birds evolved from dinosaurs; but unlike their feathered dinosaur ancestors, modern birds fly.

In geological time, using our twenty-four-hour clock, dinosaurs went extinct at about 10:45 p.m., and modern humans appeared at fifteen seconds before midnight.

You now know 82 facts about FANTASTIC DINOSAURS!

False Beliefs

Have you ever fallen for false information that's been repeated so many times you believe it simply must be true? These long-held assumptions are all erroneous. Go forth and spread the truth!

—

A mother bird will abandon her nest if you touch a baby bird. Songbirds have no sense of smell, so this myth is "for the birds."

Young George Washington was so virtuous that he could not tell a lie and confessed that he cut his father's cherry tree with a hatchet. Except this incident never happened, save in an 1806 book called *The Life of Washington the Great.*

George Washington wore wooden dentures. Wrong again. Although the president wore multiple sets of dentures, these false teeth were actually made of ivory, gold, lead, and teeth from other humans and various species of animals—including hippos!

Sweat is a healthy way to flush out toxins from your body. Sorry, but you can't "detox" through sweat any more than you can sweat actual bullets. Sweat cools off your body and keeps it from overheating.

Most of your body heat dissipates through your head so wear a hat in the winter to avoid catching a cold. Nope, the rest of your body loses as much heat per square inch as your head does. But the winter hat is still a good idea!

Deoxygenated blood is blue. This myth started because your veins are blue so therefore the blood coursing through them is blue. All human blood is red; however, an octopus is blue-blooded.

Mount Everest is the world's tallest mountain. If we're talking from base to summit, Mauna Kea in Hawaii is the winner at 33,465 feet, while puny Mount Everest is only 29,029 feet. However, nearly twenty thousand feet of Mauna Kea is below sea level while none of Mount Everest is.

Drink at least eight eight-ounce glasses of water a day. This "eight-by-eight" rule came from a 1945 report, but it also pointed out that much of this water could be obtained from the foods we eat. Staying hydrated is important, but everybody is different, so let thirst guide your water intake.

The Great Wall of China is the only man-made object visible from the moon. This space-based myth has been around since 1938—way before the Space Age. It's impossible to spot any human-made object from the moon, including the 4,500-mile-long wall that blends into its surrounding landscape.

Moths are attracted to flames. These insects use the sun and moon to navigate. When the light comes from an artificial light source such as a candle, moths become confused by the angle of light striking their eyes and spiral in toward the light and sometimes into the flame.

We only use 10 percent of our brain. Raise your hand if you're missing 90 percent of your brain. No one's sure where this myth came from, but everyone makes use of 100 percent of his or her brain.

Hair and fingernails continue to grow after death. This only happens in horror films, not real life. However, once the heart stops pumping, the skin becomes dehydrated and retracts, giving the illusion of increased hair and nail length.

Reading in dim light ruins your eyesight. Poor lighting will not cause permanent damage to your vision, but it can cause eyestrain and make your eyes tired.

Public swimming pools contain a secret chemical that turns the water a bright color when someone pees in it. No such chemical exists to surround the peeing person in a cloud of shame. Parents spread this myth to (hopefully) stop their kids from peeing in the pool.

Everyone needs eight hours of sleep per night. The amount of sleep needed changes as you age, and the ideal amount can vary from person to person. Experts recommend between fourteen to seventeen hours for newborns and on down to seven to nine hours for adults.

Your pet's mouth is cleaner than yours. Canine and feline saliva contain a higher amount of bacteria than human saliva. You brush and floss your teeth regularly to reduce the amount of bacteria in your mouth, but your pet does not.

Your pet's saliva can help heal wounds. Again, nope. A single lick can deposit millions of unfamiliar bacteria, which can cause infection.

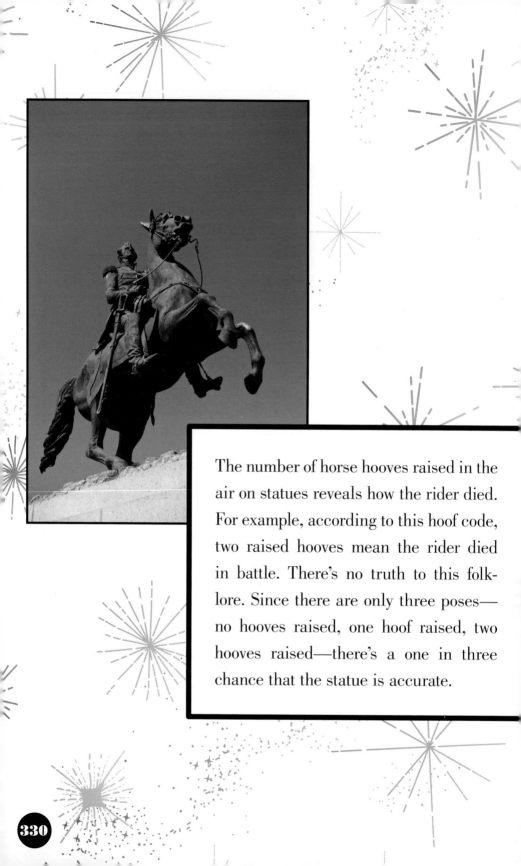

The number of horse hooves raised in the air on statues reveals how the rider died. For example, according to this hoof code, two raised hooves mean the rider died in battle. There's no truth to this folklore. Since there are only three poses—no hooves raised, one hoof raised, two hooves raised—there's a one in three chance that the statue is accurate.

You eat eight spiders a year in your sleep. Not even close—the number is zero. Sleeping humans give off vibrations that spiders find terrifying. They'd rather be hanging out in their webs or hunting for prey far away from slumbering humans.

Vomitoriums were rooms where the ancient Romans went to throw up food so they could return to the feast for seconds. These rooms did indeed exist, but they were for "vomiting out" *people,* not food; they were amphitheater passageways so spectators could enter and exit quickly.

A goldfish has a three-second memory. Goldfish actually have impressively long memories that last at least three months, according to scientific experiments.

The Scottish invented bagpipes. History sleuths traced back the origin of these wind instruments to the ancient Sumerians during the third millennium BCE.

A goal of ten thousand steps per day is necessary for good health. While walking is a terrific form of exercise, there's no recommended daily step count. The ten thousand figure came from a Japanese company that marketed its pedometer Manpo-kei, which translates to "ten thousand steps meter."

Dogs only see in black-and-white. Dogs can see the colors yellow and blue, so choose these hues when picking out toys for them.

You can't teach an old dog new tricks. It might take senior dogs longer to learn a trick than young dogs, but you can teach old dogs new tricks that they'll remember long-term.

The saying "his name is mud" came from Dr. Samuel Alexander Mudd (who conspired with John Wilkes Booth in the 1865 assassination of President Abraham Lincoln). But according to a word origin dictionary, the phrase was recorded in 1823, ten years before Mudd's birth. It's based on an obsolete sense of the word "mud" meaning "a stupid twaddling fellow."

You can eat food that fell on the floor as long as it's picked up within five seconds. Sorry, but that five-second rule doesn't hold true: No matter how fast you rescue that fallen food, bacteria will have already contaminated it.

An apple a day keeps the doctor away. Let's take a bite out of this proverb, which first appeared in a Welsh publication in 1866. There's no evidence that daily apple eating translates into fewer doctor visits.

You need to wait twenty-four hours before reporting a missing person. This is a dangerous mistaken belief. You should report a missing person case as soon as possible. Waiting twenty-four hours means valuable time is lost.

Black panthers are a separate species of big cats. No, this term actually describes coat color. A black panther can be a black-coated leopard or a dark-coated jaguar.

Sunflowers always face the sun. This fascinating phenomenon is called heliotropism and it's true for young sunflowers. However, mature sunflowers stop sun tracking and face east full-time to attract pollinating insects.

You should wait to swim after eating. Sorry, your mother was wrong. The blood supplied to aid digestion won't prevent your arm and leg muscles from properly functioning.

Cold hands, warm heart. Your hands might be cold because you're in a chilly environment. Always having cold hands is a sign of poor circulation.

Gutenberg invented the first printing press. The machine, which used movable type to print messages, was created in China more than four centuries before Johannes Gutenberg was born.

Quicksand can swallow you whole. This only happens in the movies. In real life, you'll never be swallowed by this combination of fine sand, clay, and saltwater. The human body isn't dense enough to be gobbled up by quicksand.

A grain of sand in an oyster creates a pearl. Oysters live at the bottom of the ocean, which is covered with sand, and these mollusks can rid themselves of sand. If sand made pearls, the ocean would be full of these precious gems. While about one in ten thousand oysters will form a natural pearl around a parasite, the vast majority of pearls are cultured after the oyster is seeded with a bead.

All piranhas eat flesh. The tambaqui, a piranha relative, is a vegetarian. Instead of dining on meat, this fish eats fruits that drop from overhanging trees in the Amazon.

Fortune cookies were invented in China. These treats with hidden messages actually originated in Japan. The cookies arrived in America in the early 1900s and were popular-ized by Chinese restaurants.

Tea bags were invented in Great Britain. Around 1908, a New York tea merchant sent out samples of loose tea in small silk bags. Customers dunked the bags in boiling water and this accidental invention grew in popularity.

Water drains in the opposite direction in the Southern Hemisphere. Does water rotate counterclockwise down a tub or toilet in the Northern Hemisphere and clockwise in the Southern? Whether you live above or below the equator, water drains the same.

Bananas grow on trees. Nope, the world's most popular fruit grows on the world's largest herbaceous flowering plants.

Viking helmets sported horns. No one has ever discovered a Viking-era helmet festooned with horns. A costume designer for a Wagner opera staged in the 1870s created those horned helmets.

Bulls hate the color red. It's not the color that causes bulls to charge, but rather sudden movements.

Toads cause warts if you touch them. Warts are caused by viruses, not by touching the bumpy back of a toad.

SOS stands for Save Our Ship. This international Morse code distress signal doesn't stand for anything. The SOS code is used because it's easy to tap out: three dots, three dashes, three dots.

Tomatoes are vegetables. They're fruits and part of the berry family. Fruits grow from flowers and contain seeds.

The pilgrims first landed at Plymouth Rock. In this overhyped legend, an ancestor of one of the original Mayflower passengers claimed the stone was the specific landing spot. Actually, the pilgrims first landed in what is now Provincetown, Massachusetts, in 1620, and sailed to Plymouth a month later.

Ben Franklin wanted the wild turkey as America's national symbol. This falsehood resulted from a letter Franklin wrote his daughter criticizing the bald eagle as "a bird of bad moral character" and citing the turkey as a courageous bird. But he never proposed that the turkey represent America.

Some beards contain more poop than a toilet. While beards do contain different types of bacteria, as does human skin, they don't contain feces.

Ninjas wore black. They wore clothing to blend in, not stand out. This myth likely originated with Japanese Kabuki theaters, where actors dressed in black to reflect invisibility.

The verb *unfriend* was first used in social media. *Unfriend* predates Facebook by 350 years. It was first used as a verb in the seventeenth century.

Rice thrown at weddings will expand in birds' stomachs and cause them to explode. Birdbrains have shared this myth. Rice needs to be boiled before it will expand. Besides, birds eat wild rice in fields without suffering harm, but uncooked rice can cause humans to slip and become injured.

In the letter grade system, an F has always represented failure. Back in 1897, the scores originally used an E instead of an F to mean a student had failed. But this was changed to an F when professors worried that students would believe the grade E stood for excellent.

A pound of quarters is worth more than a pound of dimes. They are equal: a pound contains two hundred dimes or eighty quarters; both equivalent to twenty dollars.

Earthquakes will destroy buildings made of cardboard. New Zealand's Transitional Cathedral is made substantially of cardboard and is designed to be earthquake-proof, fire-proof, and not turn soggy in the rain. It turns out that the flexibility of cardboard offers more strength under tension.

According to the rulebooks, only live jockeys can win horse races. In 1923, a jockey suffered a fatal heart attack while riding his horse, Sweet Kiss, in a race at Belmont Park in New York City. He remained in the saddle and crossed the finish line in first place.

Astronauts return to Earth the same height as when they blasted off. Actually, astronauts' bodies lengthen by a few inches due to the lack of gravitational forces compressing their spines. But this effect gradually disappears as gravity returns them to their original height.

When you flush an airplane toilet, the contents drop out of the bottom of the plane. While vintage airplanes had primitive toilets, such as buckets that were hurled out the window, modern aircraft have toilets that suck out waste and store it in sealed tanks. Upon landing, a truck siphons out the waste and disposes it in an underground sewage system.

Microwave ovens cause cancer. These ovens only emit microwaves when the door is shut and the oven is turned on. The amount of radiation that leaks out while heating food is far below the level that could cause harm to your health.

Walt Disney was cryogenically frozen. While Disney, who died in 1966, lives on through his films, parks, and merchandise, he wasn't frozen after his death. His family had him cremated.

Mrs. O'Leary's cow started the Great Chicago Fire. The cow was not to blame for this devastating 1871 fire. This article about a cow tipping over a lantern appeared in the *Chicago Tribune*; years later the newspaper reporter retracted his statements.

Elephants are the only mammals that can't jump. While it's true that these pachyderms can't leap off of the ground with all of their feet in the air, neither can hippos, rhinos, nor sloths.

Cats have nine lives. This myth has been around for centuries; Shakespeare even used the expression in *Romeo and Juliet*. While cats don't have multiple lives, their quick reflexes allow them to survive falls without being fatally wounded.

And then there were hoaxes that practically everyone believed until they were disproven.

1. The radio blared the news on October 30, 1938: A gigantic meteorite had smashed into a New Jersey farm. Martians were attacking New York. Thousands of panicked listeners believed they were listening to a news broadcast about an invasion from Mars. They were not. Instead they had tuned in late to a radio play narrated by Orson Welles and adapted from the sci-fi novel *The War of the Worlds.*

2. Cassius Clay (later known as Muhammad Ali) trained underwater as a teenage boxer. The only time he trained underwater was for a 1961 photo essay that appeared in *Life* magazine. Ali invented this hoax to get publicity and it worked, becoming part of his allure.

3. "Awful Calamity." "Savage Brutes at Large." The headlines in the *New York Herald* shouted these claims in 1874. This story about a mass escape of Central Park Zoo animals alleged that forty-eight people were killed and two hundred injured. Frightened readers stayed home while police grabbed their guns, but they needn't have feared—the entire story was a fabrication to draw attention to the zoo's safety practices.

4. Introducing the Canine Collection! The online fashion retailer Lyst posted that they would be selling dogs so that shoppers could complement their summer outfits with four-legged friends. There was a huge backlash on social media. The next day the marketing hoax was revealed, with the company emphasizing that dogs are not fashion accessories and drawing attention to the millions of dogs abandoned annually.

5. "Great Astronomical Discoveries Lately Made" by Sir John Herschel. The 1835 article ran in serial form on the front page of the *New York Sun*. It claimed that Herschel, a famous British astronomer, had discovered life on the moon. That was news to Herschel, who hadn't spotted any lunar creatures such as biped beavers or man bats; however, the hoax earned the *Sun* a reputation.

6. "French Invent Bathing Suit Which Melts." This urban legend appeared in 1930 newspapers, but no such water-dissolvable fabric existed.

7. When the BBC showed footage of Swiss harvesters plucking spaghetti from trees, viewers wanted to know where they could purchase their own trees. This 1957 April Fools' joke was on them.

8. In 1905, a German newspaper informed its readers that thieves had tunneled underneath the US Federal Treasury, robbing all of its silver and gold. Other papers around the world printed the news before discovering they had been duped.

9. Google always had a trick up its sleeve on April 1. In 2014, the corporation published an app that allowed users to capture Pokémon and offered a reward for the biggest collection: a job at Google as Pokémon Master. But the joke inspired some software engineers to invent the wildly popular mobile game Pokémon Go.

10. "Dogs to Be Painted White." A Copenhagen newspaper reported this new law in 1965 aimed at increasing road safety. White dogs, as opposed to black, were easily spotted at night. This hoax inspired herders in Finland to actually spray reindeer antlers with reflective paint.

11. The *Social Directory* prided itself as a listing of prominent American families, so imagine people's shock when Mr. and Mrs. F. A. von Schneider turned out to be two dachshunds. Apparently, the attorney who owned the dogs received an invitation to be included in the 1939 directory and mailed it back with the dachshunds' names.

12. *National Geographic* announced on social media that no photos of naked animals would be published. When readers clicked through to the 2016 story, they saw photographs of dressed-up puppies and kittens from the early 1900s along with "April Fools!"

13. The first April Fools' Day hoax on record occurred in 1698. Tourists were instructed to enter the white gate at the Tower of London to view the annual ceremony of washing the lions. Neither a white gate nor lion bath awaited, but the prank continued year after year.

You now know 77 facts about FALSE BELIEFS!

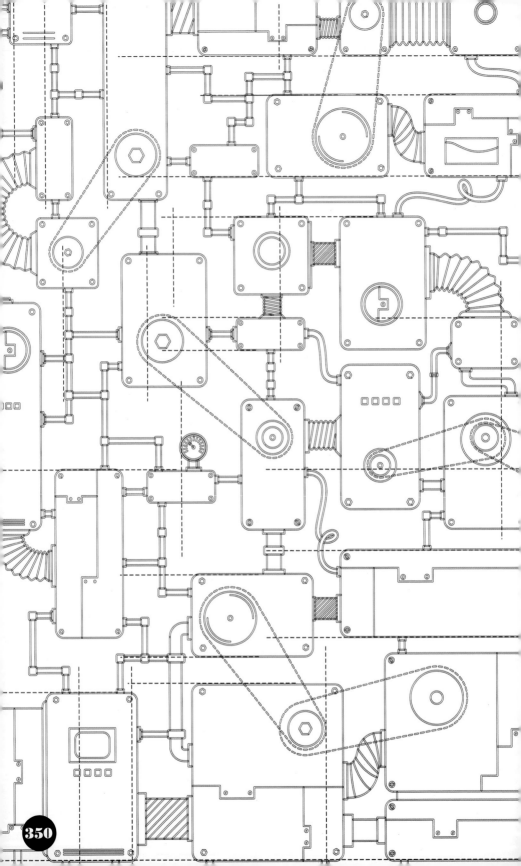

Absurd Technology and Machines

When people bring their ideas to life, sometimes the resulting technology and machines can be bizarre.

—

How did scientists use satellite technology to identify emperor penguin colonies from space? They searched for poop stains on the ice at Antarctic breeding sites.

A bottlenose dolphin named Merlin displays his own brand of magic by using an iPad to communicate with scientists. First Merlin is shown real objects such as a plastic duck; then the dolphin touches the photos of those objects on the screen.

Researchers used an echolocation beam transmitted by a dolphin to obtain an image of what the dolphin saw: a submerged man. The echo signal was captured by a hydrophone system and then computer-enhanced at a sound imaging lab.

Grooves along a stretch of New Mexico's Route 66 are designed to play "America the Beautiful." The grooves work like rumble strips and play different pitches as a car drives over them, but only if the driver obeys the forty-five mile per hour speed limit.

NASA held a contest to discover the best spacesuit design for *Apollo 11* astronauts. The suits needed to protect the astronauts from solar radiation and searing heat, and had to supply oxygen, control temperatures via an adjustable thermostat, and be comfortable and flexible to allow movement. But the winner wasn't a top engineering firm; instead Playtex, the bra and girdle company, won with their design!

Now NASA is holding a "Lunar Loo Challenge" that's open to the public. This competition is for the best space toilet for astronauts to use on a future trip to the moon, tentatively scheduled for 2024. The design must be able to accommodate women as well as men since this will be the first time a woman will step onto the moon's surface.

A video went viral showing metal pieces fitting together so precisely that the end result seemed to be one seamless block of metal. The clip wasn't produced using special effects; instead, it demonstrated a Chinese company's high-precision machine that creates miniature parts with features finer than a micron—about the thickness of a human red blood cell.

"A Car that Flies. A Plane that Drives." That's the aim of PAL-V, which stands for Personal Air and Land Vehicle, founded in 2008. The world's first commercial flying car should soon be spotted on land and in the air.

A flying hoverboard achieved a world record by traveling a total distance of 905 feet, 2 inches.

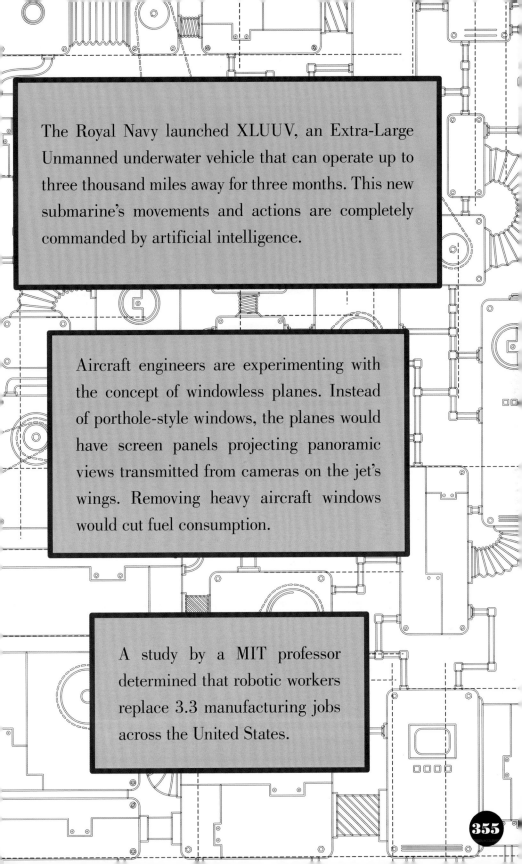

The Royal Navy launched XLUUV, an Extra-Large Unmanned underwater vehicle that can operate up to three thousand miles away for three months. This new submarine's movements and actions are completely commanded by artificial intelligence.

Aircraft engineers are experimenting with the concept of windowless planes. Instead of porthole-style windows, the planes would have screen panels projecting panoramic views transmitted from cameras on the jet's wings. Removing heavy aircraft windows would cut fuel consumption.

A study by a MIT professor determined that robotic workers replace 3.3 manufacturing jobs across the United States.

About 70 percent of robots work in four manufacturing industries: automakers, electronics, plastics and chemical, and metals.

The world's first automated DNA testing lab opened in San Francisco, California. Robots perform all the work, processing thousands of samples a day with high precision.

A study predicts that by 2030 up to eight hundred million global workers will be replaced by robotic automation. The occupations hardest hit will be food workers and machine operators.

Can a chatbot, a human-mimicking program, fool judges? In the annual Loebner Prize competition, judges must determine whether they're chatting with a person or a computer program. The prize goes to the most human-like chatbot.

Robotic companion pets are keeping elderly Americans company. These cats and dogs are part of a loneliness intervention program. The robots make sounds and gestures that mimic real pets, such as meowing and stretching.

The Canadarm, a robotic arm constructed in Canada, worked aboard US space shuttle missions for thirty years. It was designed to work in a weightless environment and could lift more than sixty-six thousand pounds using less electricity than a teakettle.

Wearable technology, or wearables, has taken off, with new products constantly being introduced. They've come a long way since the first clunky prototypes.

1. Today, people wear miniature computers with sensors that collect data. Smart watches can track fitness, provide entertainment, display maps, function as mobile phones, and more. One company claims that wearing its smart watch could add two years to your life by increasing physical activity.

2. Smart clothing technology can help you perfect your yoga poses, collect data from your socks to improve your walking and running techniques, and alert you from a swimsuit sensor when you need to apply more sunscreen.

3. Smart glasses have integrated cameras and microphones. You can snap 3-D photos and shoot videos, enjoy music, answer phone calls, and even relax and focus your mind—all while wearing glasses.

4. Exoskeletons, robotic suits that humans wear, can help people perform physically demanding tasks while reducing injuries; they can also aid in physical therapy.

5. New exoskeletons will use artificial intelligence technology to help people climb stairs, avoid obstacles, and navigate terrain.

6. Bioengineers are experimenting with 3-D printing to build living tissues, with an eye toward printing replacement organs.

7. A brain-machine interface company is working on creating a chip that can be implanted to help people with severe brain injuries and diseases. Then humans will be able to merge with artificial intelligence.

8. Small video cameras attached to helmets capture the action of extreme sports such as skydiving, surfing, bungee jumping, and caving.

9. Players wearing virtual reality headsets and walking on a special 360-degree treadmill will be able to navigate inside their favorite videogames. The combination will allow players to roam around virtual worlds and burn calories while gaming.

10. Another virtual reality gaming system is geared toward children with physical disabilities. The program aims to transform exercise therapy through games that participants can play from their bed or wheelchair.

11. Scientists are developing smart contact lenses that will treat glaucoma, zoom in on faraway objects, and provide a wide range of information using built-in LCD displays.

12. Smart hearing aids can be controlled via a smartphone, allowing users to hear music and audio more clearly.

13. Health sensors can monitor vital signs such as blood pressure and body temperature. These smart patches can send information wirelessly to a monitoring system that will alert doctors of any declines in a patient's condition.

14. Wearable jewelry can detect epileptic seizures and alert caregivers via a smartphone.

15. Another wearable device displays data about a person's sleeping patterns. These sleep trackers remain on the sleeper all night and then analyze the results.

16. Medical alert systems with built-in GPS can be used to locate young children, seniors with dementia, and lost pets.

17. A smart safety vest designed for roadside construction workers uses GPS to track workers' movements and warn if a crash is about to occur.

18. A smart safety cycling helmet is designed with lights, turn signals, and SOS alert technology to send an emergency message and a GPS location in the event of a fall.

19. The ultimate wearable? It's a microchip that a Wisconsin company implants in workers' hands. This voluntary option allows employees to check themselves out at the company's break room, use machines, open doors, and log in to computers.

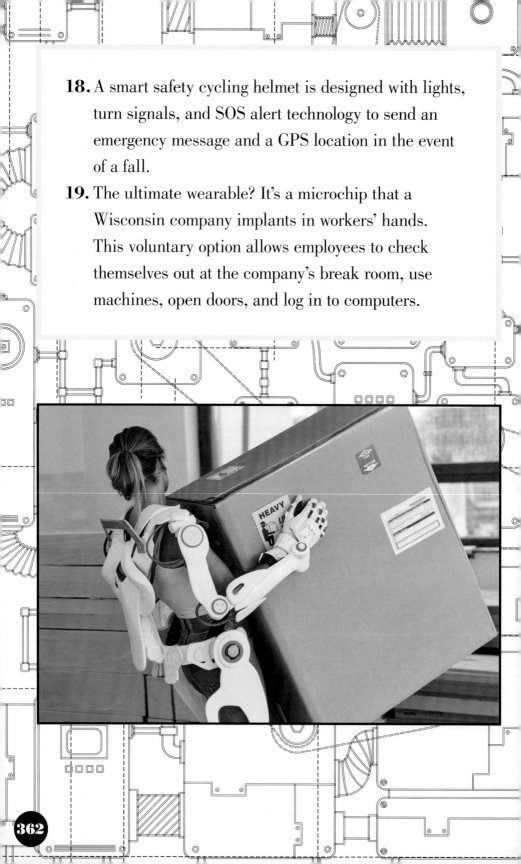

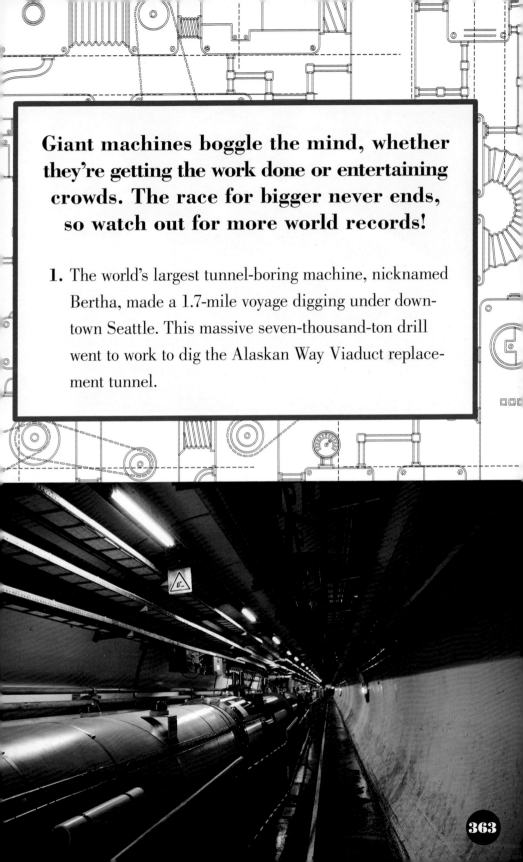

Giant machines boggle the mind, whether they're getting the work done or entertaining crowds. The race for bigger never ends, so watch out for more world records!

1. The world's largest tunnel-boring machine, nicknamed Bertha, made a 1.7-mile voyage digging under downtown Seattle. This massive seven-thousand-ton drill went to work to dig the Alaskan Way Viaduct replacement tunnel.

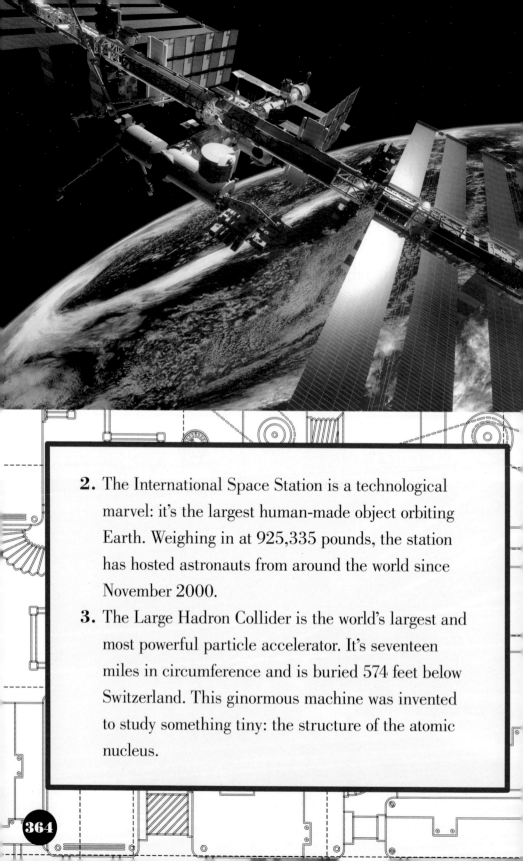

2. The International Space Station is a technological marvel: it's the largest human-made object orbiting Earth. Weighing in at 925,335 pounds, the station has hosted astronauts from around the world since November 2000.

3. The Large Hadron Collider is the world's largest and most powerful particle accelerator. It's seventeen miles in circumference and is buried 574 feet below Switzerland. This ginormous machine was invented to study something tiny: the structure of the atomic nucleus.

4. Scientists plan to build a new underground accelerator that would be three times larger than the Large Hadron Collider.

5. Meanwhile, above ground, the giant bucket-wheel excavator is the biggest land-based vehicle in the world. Weighing in at more than thirty-one million pounds, this machine can dig daily holes the length of a football field and more than eighty feet deep.

6. Imagine a thirty-seven-ton spider crawling down the street before climbing a building! La Princesse, a gigantic mechanical spider that stands fifty feet high, awed the crowds in Liverpool, England, while managing to terrify people who have arachnophobia.

7. In another piece of street theater, the Sultan's Elephant lumbered through London. This mechanical elephant weighed forty-two tons—as much as seven African elephants!

8. The world's largest capsule vending machine is on display in a shopping mall in Malaysia. It stands fifteen feet, five inches tall and contains prizes for shoppers to win.

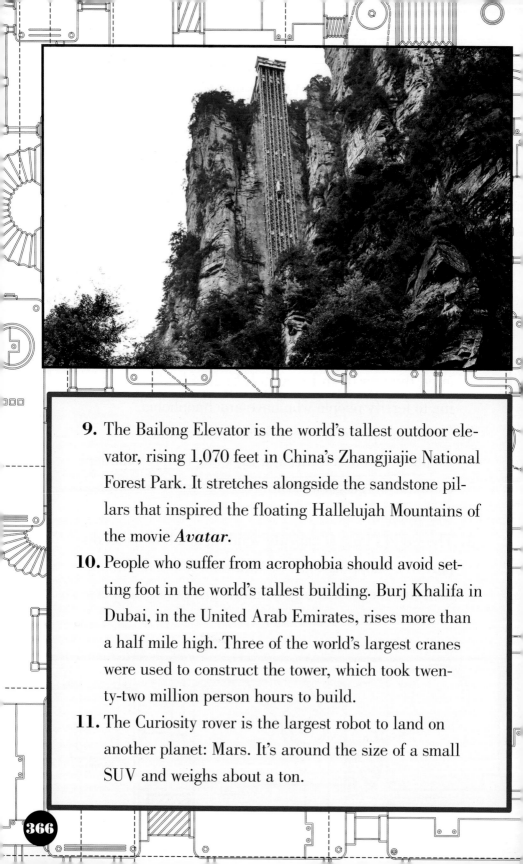

9. The Bailong Elevator is the world's tallest outdoor elevator, rising 1,070 feet in China's Zhangjiajie National Forest Park. It stretches alongside the sandstone pillars that inspired the floating Hallelujah Mountains of the movie *Avatar*.

10. People who suffer from acrophobia should avoid setting foot in the world's tallest building. Burj Khalifa in Dubai, in the United Arab Emirates, rises more than a half mile high. Three of the world's largest cranes were used to construct the tower, which took twenty-two million person hours to build.

11. The Curiosity rover is the largest robot to land on another planet: Mars. It's around the size of a small SUV and weighs about a ton.

12. The world's most powerful x-ray telescope, the Chandra X-ray Observatory, allows scientists around the world to understand the structure and evolution of our universe.

13. One of the world's first computers and data centers was humongous. The Electronic Numerical Integrator and Computer weighed thirty tons and took up an entire room. This great-great grandparent of today's machines was invented in 1946.

14. Most magnetic resonance imaging (MRI) machines are large tube-shaped magnets to create detailed body images. But the world's most powerful MRI is equipped with a superconducting magnet strong enough to lift a sixty-six-ton battle tank!

15. Big Bike weighs more than 5.5 tons and is the biggest two-wheeled contraption in the world. This snazzy red and gray cycle measures sixteen feet, eight inches high. But how does the rider reach those very extended handlebars?

16. The Stratolaunch aircraft is the world's largest plane with its 385-foot wingspan, wider than a National Football League field. This behemoth uses six engines to lift off the ground and was designed to launch satellites into orbit.

17. The largest vessel in the world, The Prelude, is a floating natural gas facility. It stretches nearly one-third of a mile long and boasts storage tanks that could fill 175 Olympic-size swimming pools. This

vessel can harvest enough natural gas to power Hong Kong, China, for one year.

18. The biggest dump truck is a huge monster with the combined power of seventeen heavy-duty pickup trucks. The Belaz 75710 moves rocks at a Siberian coal mine.

19. A big machine needs a big crane to move it around, and the Taisun Crane in China fits the bill. It holds the record as the world's strongest crane, capable of lifting more than forty-four million pounds.

You can 3-D print practically anything now, including food. A kitchen appliance called Foodini prints using edible ingredients squeezed out of capsules. This machine is advertised as a "mini food manufacturing plant shrunk down to the size of an oven."

The Third Thumb is a 3-D-printed robotic digit that researchers tested to find out how fast the brain adapts to body augmentation. Participants quickly learned to master their robotic thumb. This research could change the way we design human prosthetics.

Bio 3-D printers can craft living human tissues into bone, cartilage, and muscle. Once the structures are alive and growing they can be implanted in patients.

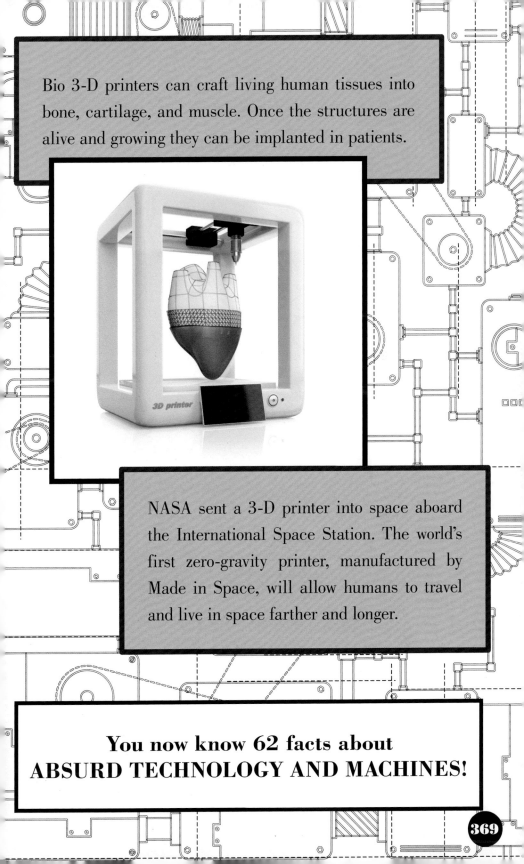

NASA sent a 3-D printer into space aboard the International Space Station. The world's first zero-gravity printer, manufactured by Made in Space, will allow humans to travel and live in space farther and longer.

You now know 62 facts about
ABSURD TECHNOLOGY AND MACHINES!

Oddball Animal Friends

Wouldn't it be boring if all your friends were alike? Extraordinary friendships between animals of different species prove that BFFs come in all colors, shapes, and sizes.

—

When a tiny Chihuahua puppy named Lundy arrived at the Mia Foundation, an unlikely bond formed between Lundy and a pigeon named Herman. Both animals faced physical challenges: Lundy couldn't walk and Herman couldn't fly. But that didn't stop Herman from taking Lundy under his wing and the two cuddled together.

While out on her walk, Staffordshire bull terrier Peggy found an abandoned magpie and adopted the bird. Peggy even started producing milk to feed the magpie, whom she treated as her own puppy! The two friends hung out from the moment they awoke until they went to sleep.

Lions and tigers and bears, oh my! This trio—Leo the African lion, Shere Khan the Bengal tiger, and Baloo the black bear—was rescued by police officers from a basement. All three cubs were only a few months old and terrified. They were brought to an animal sanctuary in Georgia, where the "brothers from different mothers" remained inseparable.

After a surrogate mother cat finished feeding her foster kittens, she still had milk to spare. And along came eight orphaned baby hedgehogs. Musya adopted this litter of hungry, prickly babies too!

A common merganser earned the title "super mom of the year" when a photographer spotted her on a Minnesota lake with fifty-six ducklings in tow. Typical females hatch eight to eleven eggs, so the brood traveling behind this mother was a mixed family.

When Asian elephant Tarra retired from a life in show biz, she became the first resident at the Elephant Sanctuary. There, every elephant was paired with a female gal pal, but Tarra never found her special friend. That is until stray dog Bella arrived on the scene and an immediate bond formed. The two were so close that when Bella needed surgery, Tarra held vigil until her canine friend recuperated.

Labrador retriever Lisha never gave birth to puppies, but she became a surrogate mother to more than thirty orphaned animals at a South African wildlife reserve. When Lisha spots a box, she automatically assumes that it's time to mother a new creature: everything from a porcupine to a pygmy hippo.

Another dog adopted three white Bengal tiger cubs after their mother rejected the trio. Golden retriever Isabella's puppies were weaned and she had plenty of milk to spare for the newborn cubs. The dog cuddled and nursed Nasira, Anjika, and Sidani at the wildlife park where they all lived.

Baby hippo Owen lost his mother when a tsunami slammed into the coast of Africa. Villagers rescued Owen and brought him to an animal sanctuary, where the terrified 600-pound hippo cowered behind a 130-year-old giant tortoise named Mzee. The grumpy grandfather grew fond of his adopted grandson, and the duo swam, ate, played, and slept together.

An orphaned litter of Eastern cottontail bunnies needed a spot to snuggle at the wildlife rehab center. They discovered their own private featherbed: Noah, a one-legged homing pigeon, who hugs the rabbits with his wings.

Plucky rodent Rattus befriended Shenna the African leopard for lunchtime. While the rat gobbled some scraps, the big cat sniffed the bold brown rat.

In an odd pairing at a Japanese zoo, squirrel monkeys and capybaras share the same enclosure even though their paths don't cross in the wild. The world's biggest rodents allow the monkeys to ride piggyback.

An accidental friendship formed at another Japanese zoo. A tiny dwarf hamster named Gohan was presented to rat snake Aochan as a snack. But the snake preferred to make friends with the rodent and the pair shared a cage.

A monkey and a pigeon don't have much in common, but that didn't stop an abandoned baby macaque from clinging to a white pigeon. The adorable duo struck up an unusual friendship at an animal sanctuary.

Two pairs of abandoned babies—Sumatran tiger cubs and orangutans—became playmates in an animal hospital. The endangered species would be deadly enemies in the wild, but they formed a fabulous foursome in their nursery.

Over the years, chimpanzee Anjana watched her human caregiver raising baby animals at the sanctuary where the chimp has lived since birth. Anjana polished her own mothering skills when a hurricane flooded the sanctuary and two white tiger cubs had to be separated from their stressed mother. The copycat chimp bottle-fed the cubs and helped raise them.

Once a farm cat weaned her litter of kittens, she began to nurse a new litter of little stinkers. The farmer placed six abandoned baby skunks with his cat. After her motherly instincts launched, the cat carried around her adopted striped babies to show them off.

They should be predator and prey, but a lioness called Kamunyak who roams a wildlife reserve keeps befriending oryxes. Since the calves never fled from the lioness, her hunting behavior didn't kick in.

Snuggled in with a mother dachshund's litter of tan puppies was one pink standout: a piglet! Pink was born premature and had a difficult time nursing alongside the other eleven piglets so the farmer moved him into the house. Tink the dog welcomed her new baby and polished his pink skin with her tongue.

Two big cats were rescued from a roadside zoo where they were used to breed ligers—the offspring of a male lion and a tigress. Lions and tigers don't breed together in the wild; ligers suffer from excessive birth defects. Big Cat Rescue spayed Zabu the white tigress and neutered Cameron the lion, and the cats ran, played, and swam side by side.

The author's adopted dog, Splash, with his winning personality, was an ambassador for the misunderstood Rottweiler breed and became fast friends with rescued rabbit Scooby Doo. The dynamic duo stopped traffic when they napped together on a sunny deck!

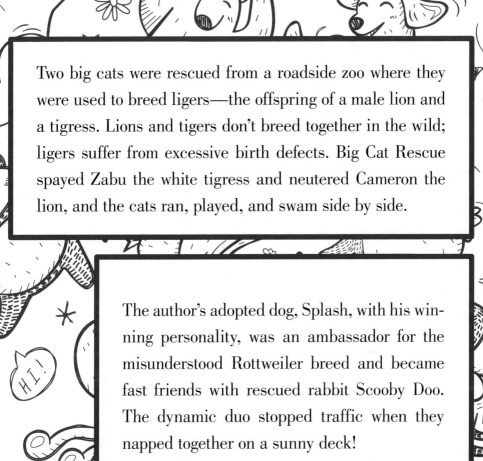

Ella the rescue pig is bursting with mischief—she eats homework and opens containers while rooting for food. Fortunately, her family's adopted duckling, Miracle, follows Ella everywhere, keeping her from becoming too naughty.

Chowder the potbellied pig thinks he's a dog, perhaps because he shares his home with five canine siblings. He especially loves to photobomb group shots and share spoonfuls of peanut butter!

After the orangutan Tonda lost her mate, the elderly great ape became depressed. But she perked right up when zookeepers brought her a stray tabby kitten they named TK. Her kitty pal kept Tonda young and she lived to the ripe age of fifty.

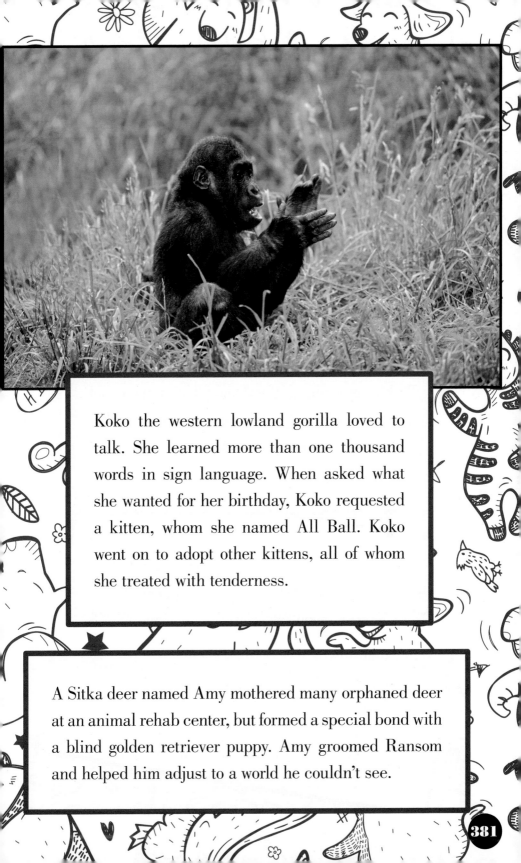

Koko the western lowland gorilla loved to talk. She learned more than one thousand words in sign language. When asked what she wanted for her birthday, Koko requested a kitten, whom she named All Ball. Koko went on to adopt other kittens, all of whom she treated with tenderness.

A Sitka deer named Amy mothered many orphaned deer at an animal rehab center, but formed a special bond with a blind golden retriever puppy. Amy groomed Ransom and helped him adjust to a world he couldn't see.

Capuchin monkeys living in Brazil adopted and raised a baby marmoset. Even though the mother monkeys were a different species, they nursed the baby and carried her on their backs.

Proving that opposites attract, a senior basset hound named Beryl was joined by tawny owl Wol every evening. Beryl snuggled on the couch and Wol perched on her back as they watched nature documentaries on TV.

An early bond formed between Anthony and Riley. The lion and coyote were both around one month old when they were brought to an Arizona animal sanctuary. Both species are social animals, and even when the lion quickly outgrew the coyote, their close link continued.

Brant geese mate for life, but what happens when a male goose chooses a forty-five-year-old female Aldabra tortoise as his partner? This odd couple clicked: the goose protected the tortoise, following her everywhere, while the tortoise nabbed the best spot at the all-you-can-eat salad bar.

Cute orphans Lulu the fox and Humbug the badger arrived at a wildlife sanctuary in England. The unlikely duo drank from their baby bottles and then tumbled together during energetic play sessions.

JoeJoe the capybara had an enormous personality as a social media star. This popular giant rodent loved babysitting buddies of different species: cuddling with husky puppies, swimming with ducklings, and letting chicks parade on his back.

Pippin and Kate bounced around like playful siblings, but one was a fawn and the other was a Great Dane. Then they snuggled together on the grass with their necks curled around each other.

Aren't cats and rats sworn enemies? Ranj the orange tabby shattered that stereotype with his pal Peanut. The rat shadowed the cat and crawled all over him, and both friends groomed each other.

Juniper used Moose as a comfy couch. The pet fox claimed the Australian shepherd mix as her faithful sidekick. The two pals dine together, tails wagging in tandem.

Mäuschen, an eight-hundred-pound Asiatic black bear, welcomed a stray cat into her enclosure at the Berlin Zoo. The cat made herself at home, seeking shelter between the paws of the huge bear, who protected her pet kitty.

Racehorses can be high-strung, so they're matched up with companion ponies who keep them calm. But Strong Impact, a thoroughbred at Belmont Park, had an unusual barnyard buddy. Charlie the pig trotted through the barn and chose Strong Impact and acted as the horse's security blanket.

When an outgoing pit bull named Oakley befriended cantankerous donkey Wendell, magic happened. The two chased each other and did happy zoomies together.

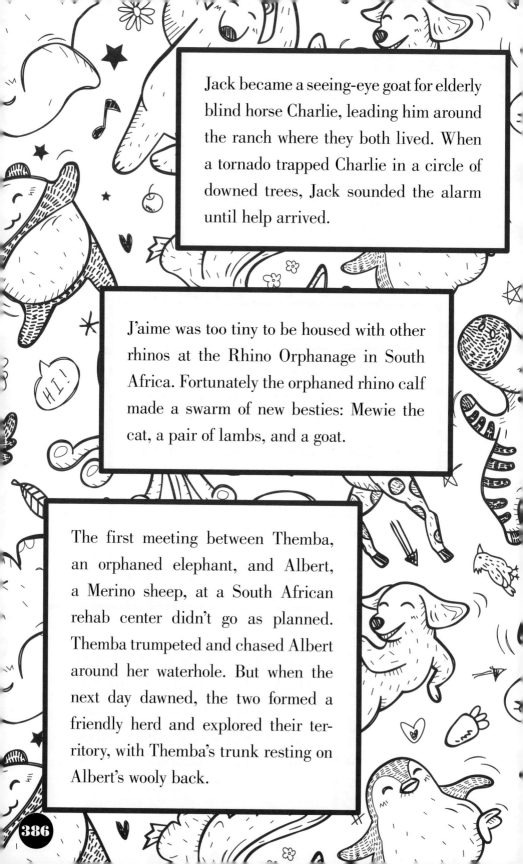

Jack became a seeing-eye goat for elderly blind horse Charlie, leading him around the ranch where they both lived. When a tornado trapped Charlie in a circle of downed trees, Jack sounded the alarm until help arrived.

J'aime was too tiny to be housed with other rhinos at the Rhino Orphanage in South Africa. Fortunately the orphaned rhino calf made a swarm of new besties: Mewie the cat, a pair of lambs, and a goat.

The first meeting between Themba, an orphaned elephant, and Albert, a Merino sheep, at a South African rehab center didn't go as planned. Themba trumpeted and chased Albert around her waterhole. But when the next day dawned, the two formed a friendly herd and explored their territory, with Themba's trunk resting on Albert's wooly back.

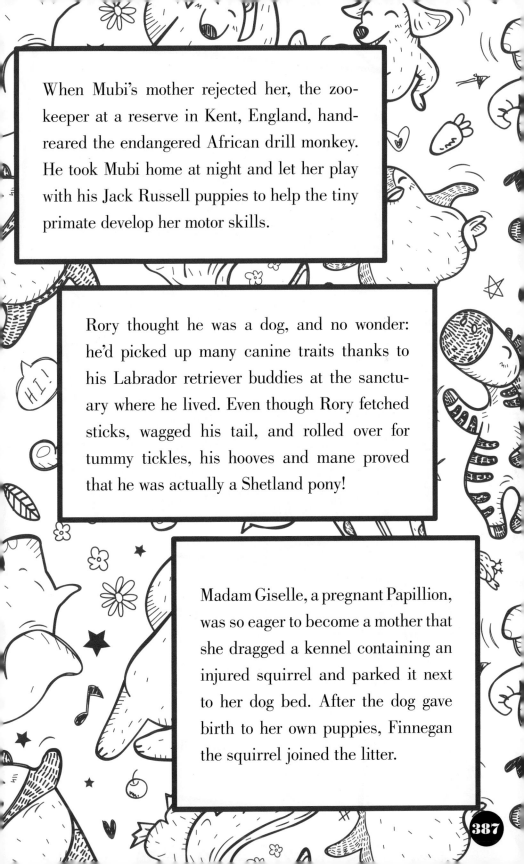

When Mubi's mother rejected her, the zoo-keeper at a reserve in Kent, England, hand-reared the endangered African drill monkey. He took Mubi home at night and let her play with his Jack Russell puppies to help the tiny primate develop her motor skills.

Rory thought he was a dog, and no wonder: he'd picked up many canine traits thanks to his Labrador retriever buddies at the sanctuary where he lived. Even though Rory fetched sticks, wagged his tail, and rolled over for tummy tickles, his hooves and mane proved that he was actually a Shetland pony!

Madam Giselle, a pregnant Papillion, was so eager to become a mother that she dragged a kennel containing an injured squirrel and parked it next to her dog bed. After the dog gave birth to her own puppies, Finnegan the squirrel joined the litter.

After a tiny stray kitten showed up in a Massachusetts backyard, the homeowners discovered that she already had a caregiver: a crow! Moses the crow fed bugs to Cassie the kitten and protected her from other animals. Even after the feline finally became a housecat, the crow pecked at the door until Cassie came out to play.

Simon Cow-ell was supposed to join other cows at a Thailand sanctuary, but the cow had another plan. As he recovered from losing part of his hind leg, Simon met a friend of another species: an African spurred tortoise named Leonardo. The cow followed the tortoise everywhere and even used Leonardo's shell as his personal pillow.

Maybe it was their matching elongated necks that attracted Wilma the ostrich to Bea the giraffe. The two live at Busch Gardens and roam the Serengeti Plain together. The ostrich isn't fazed when Bea uses her tongue to explore Wilma's beak.

A suckling piglet joined a heap of wiggly Rottweiler puppies after her mother rejected her. Apple Sauce was the runt and near death when the pig farmer put the piglet in with the puppies. The mama Rottie, Sasha, immediately started nursing Apple Sauce.

Bubbles the African elephant and Bella the Labrador retriever both went wild for water play. Despite their extreme size difference, the duo invented games to play in a safari reserve's pool. Bubbles tossed a ball using her trunk, and Bella used Bubbles as a diving board to fetch the ball!

Like the duo in *The Fox and the Hound* movie, Tinni the dog and Sniffer the wild fox romp and play in the Norwegian forests.

The idea was to nurse an abandoned greyhound back to health at a wildlife sanctuary and then find her an adoptive home. But Jasmine wiggled into a new job and never left. She became a full-time foster mother to an amazing assortment of orphaned and abandoned animals: a roe deer fawn, fox cubs, badger cubs, chicks, guinea pigs, puppies, and rabbits.

The friendship was on after Bixby invited Harry P. Otter into his den to play with his collection of stuffed animals. The beaver and the river otter became fast friends at a nature center, swimming alongside each other in a big pond.

Sahara the cheetah and Alexa the Anatolian shepherd worked together as ambassadors for a conservation program. They toured schools to raise awareness for saving the cheetah population from extinction.

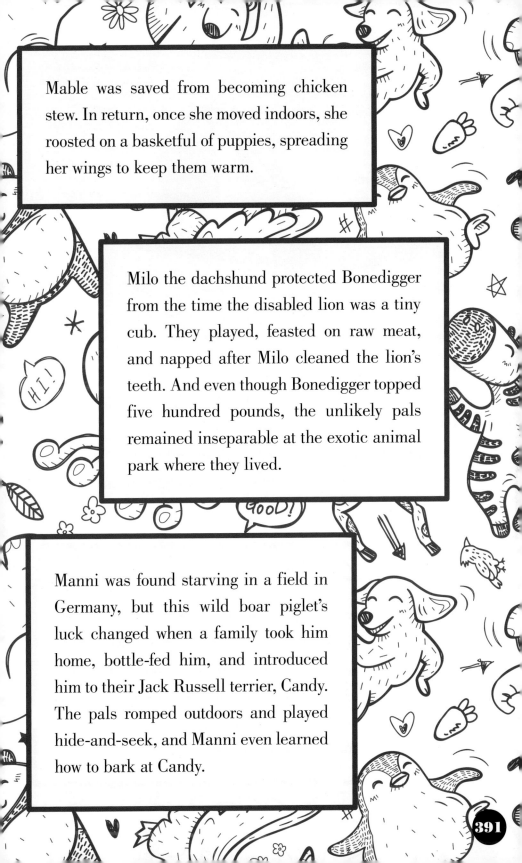

Mable was saved from becoming chicken stew. In return, once she moved indoors, she roosted on a basketful of puppies, spreading her wings to keep them warm.

Milo the dachshund protected Bonedigger from the time the disabled lion was a tiny cub. They played, feasted on raw meat, and napped after Milo cleaned the lion's teeth. And even though Bonedigger topped five hundred pounds, the unlikely pals remained inseparable at the exotic animal park where they lived.

Manni was found starving in a field in Germany, but this wild boar piglet's luck changed when a family took him home, bottle-fed him, and introduced him to their Jack Russell terrier, Candy. The pals romped outdoors and played hide-and-seek, and Manni even learned how to bark at Candy.

Jet the dolphin and Miri the seal chased each other around a marine park in Australia. These underwater pals would have competed for fish in the wild, but in the pool they became inseparable. They even developed their own language: Miri barked and Jet clicked back!

They met cute: orangutan Suryia rode atop Bubbles the elephant with her handlers to cool off in the river when suddenly a stray dog appeared. The hound, Roscoe, joined in and never left the wildlife preserve. Suryia and Roscoe formed a fast friendship, playing, hugging, swimming, and sharing bananas.

The SPCA in Bucks County, Pennsylvania, rescued Hemingway the goose and Waffles the mini horse from an outdoor paddock. They got adopted together, and Hemingway continued to protect Waffles on their new farm.

After June the baby raccoon was rescued and rehabbed, she was supposed to be released back into the wild. However, the spoiled raccoon decided she preferred her air-conditioned house. When the family added a dog to the mix, June welcomed Waffles, and the two wrestled and got into mischief together.

When an orphaned baby rhino named Clover arrived at a nature preserve in South Africa, he felt confused until he spied a goat through a fence on a neighboring farm. Then Bok-Bok made Clover feel right at home, acting as the rhino's nanny.

Boxer Billy took on a paternal role caring for an abandoned baby goat called Lilly. He protected the tiny kid and even cleaned her mouth after she ate.

On a farm in Germany, Rhodesian ridgeback Katjinga mothered a tiny Vietnamese piglet named Paulinchen. After a few days, the dog even started producing milk for the wrinkly abandoned pig.

Two orphaned babies—wombat Wally and kangaroo Buggy—became inseparable at an Australian rescue, cuddling in the same pouch and spooning in front of the fireplace.

Bull terrier Nino became a watchful big brother the instant he met Rillette and kept a watchful eye on the tiny gosling. Rillette grew larger and the duo chased each other around the garden until Nino decided to take a nap. But the goose had other plans: she walked all over the dog to wake him up and then honked with laughter.

Things started off a tad bumpy when Safi met Wister. The German shepherd mix approached the donkey at the ranch where they lived. Wister tried to kick Safi, and the dog got the message. They tried again, this time with a fence separating them, and the pair took naps and hiked together.

Golden retriever Chino ignored other dogs, but a fish mesmerized him! Chino got up close and personal with a koi named Falstaff who lived in a backyard pond. The huge orange and black fish would nibble on the dog's paws and was rewarded with food pellets.

Sharky the pit bull became famous on social media for his fondness of all creatures. The big dog's eyes sparkled when he spotted chicks, a Siamese cat, a potbellied pig, guinea pigs, and rabbits, all of whom shared his house. Millions of people viewed videos of Sharky cuddling with his critter crew and letting chicks climb all over him.

It was a shaggy dog story: Joker traveled every day to Dolphin Reef in Israel to swim with a pod of bottlenose dolphins. The furry pooch and his aquatic playmates frolicked together in the sea as the dolphins swam around Joker and splashed him with their tails.

After tumbling into a well, an elephant calf became separated from his herd. Jotto was rescued and taken to an elephant orphanage in Kenya where he met Pea, an ostrich who thought she was an elephant. Pea became Jotto's feathery pillow.

A pet African goose named Buttons took blind boxer Bak under her wing, leading his canine buddy around the farm in Poland where they both live. Buttons honks and Bak follows.

Dotty's mother rejected her speckled baby, but the tiny lamb was in luck. She was born on an Australian farm that bred Dalmatians and one female named Zoe mothered the lamb. The spotty flock of two blended together.

Gerald the giraffe needed a pal to keep him company while he waited for a mate at a zoo in England. Even though Eddie had a different perspective on life, Gerald immediately welcomed the goat as his best mate. Eddie even climbed onto Gerald's neck to cuddle!

Crouton the African sulcata tortoise cherished her heating blanket at the animal refuge she shared with a variety of species. But the tortoise abandoned her blankie to bury herself in a warm puppy pile.

The owlet and the pussycat met when they were both around one month old. Curious black kitten Fum leapt straight up to greet barn owl Gebra in midflight. The cat joined his feathered friend in a fig tree, high-fiving the owl. The falconer in Spain who raised these unlikely friends took videos that went viral.

Boonlua lost both legs and an arm when he was attacked by a pack of dogs in Thailand. The long-tailed macaque dragged himself to a temple, where he got help. Then the special-needs primate moved into an elephant sanctuary, but he was lonely. In hopped some furry friends—rabbits and a guinea pig—and Boonlua enjoyed grooming them and nabbing treats from their bowls.

When a critically endangered black rhino was born, the staff at a wildlife sanctuary in Kenya hand-raised the baby after his blind mother neglected him. In a few days Omni met another orphan—Digby, a warthog. The two became brothers in spirit: Digby groomed Omni and gobbled up pesky ticks, and each night the warthog slept atop the rhino.

One of the world's smallest horses, Einstein, weighed only six pounds and measured fourteen inches tall at birth. This mini miniature pinto colt had hooves the size of a quarter! Einstein was too tiny to frolic with the other colts, so he searched for the perfect playmates and found Saint Bernard Hannah and boxer Lilly.

**You now know 77 facts about
ODDBALL ANIMAL FRIENDS!**

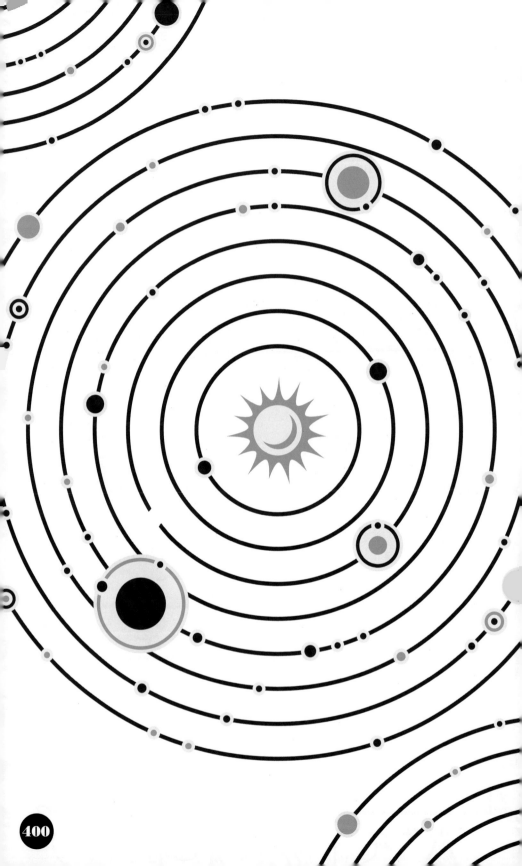

Peculiar Planets and Mysterious Moons

Eight amazing planets—each one incredibly different—call our solar system home. Earth has a moon that orbits our home planet, but more than two hundred moons orbit other planets and asteroids. Astronomers are constantly discovering out-of-this world information about our solar system.

—

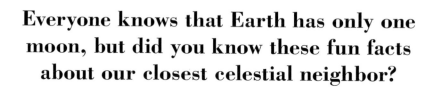

Everyone knows that Earth has only one moon, but did you know these fun facts about our closest celestial neighbor?

1. The first astronaut to walk on the moon was Neil Armstrong, in 1969. A human hasn't walked on the moon since 1972, when *Apollo 17* completed its final mission. In total, twelve humans have walked on the moon.
2. NASA plans to send the next man and the first woman to the moon by 2024 during the Artemis program.
3. The moon formed around 4.45 billion years ago, when a small planet the size of Mars struck Earth. The impact sent large amounts of debris into orbit that clumped together and formed the moon. Therefore, the moon is a broken-off piece of a young planet Earth!

4. Why do the moon and sun appear to be roughly the same size in the sky when the moon is actually 400 times smaller than the sun? That's because the moon is 400 times closer to Earth than the sun. The sun is ninety-three million miles away, but the moon is only 239,000 miles away from Earth.

5. As the moon's interior cools, it shrinks and gets wrinkles. Scientists believe that the moon has shrunk about 150 feet over the last several hundred million years, and that this shrinking could be producing moonquakes.

6. The International Astronomical Union (IAU) has rules for naming the moon's craters. The IAU assigns names from deceased American astronauts and Russian cosmonauts along with deceased artists, explorers, scholars, and scientists.

7. While Eugene Shoemaker received the National Medal of Science, one dream eluded him. While he hoped to be the first geologist to walk on the moon, he was disqualified after being diagnosed with Addison's disease. However, after he died, some of his ashes were carried to the moon by the *Lunar Prospector* space probe, making Shoemaker the only person to receive a lunar burial.

8. Each night the moon appears to change shape. It goes through eight different phases: from new moon (invisible from Earth) to full moon (completely illuminated). Of course, the moon isn't actually changing shape: it's our view of the moon that's altering as the sun lights up different parts.

9. The full moon can appear different each time. A blood moon occurs during a total lunar eclipse, when the moon glows red. A blue moon isn't named for the hue; instead it's a rare "extra" moon during a season with four full moons. A bright harvest moon rises during the beginning of autumn.

10. A supermoon looks larger than a typical full moon; that's because the moon is at its closest point in its orbit around Earth.

11. Earthlings can only spot 60 percent of the moon's surface. The same side of the moon always faces Earth and is known as the "near side."

12. The "far side" of the moon—the part that faces away from Earth—was only imaged in 1959. That's when the *Soviet Luna 3* spacecraft flew past and took twenty-nine photographs, giving us the first glimpse of the far side.

13. The moon has temperature swings. When sunlight hits its surface, the temperature can rise to a scorching 260°F. But when the sun sets, temperatures can dip down to -280°F.

14. More than 842 pounds of lunar rocks and soil accompanied *Apollo* astronauts back to Earth.

15. Our moon is Earth's only natural satellite. It has neither rings nor moons of its own.

16. The moon is the fifth largest moon in the solar system.

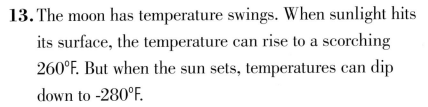

Up until 1610, humans never knew that other moons existed. That's when Italian astronomer Galileo Galilei made improvements to his telescope and discovered the four biggest moons of Jupiter.

Our solar system contains more than two hundred moons . . . and counting, as scientists continue to discover more.

It's possible for moons to have moons of their own, according to some astronomers, although they have yet to prove that these pet moons exist. People have invented a colorful assortment of names, including *moonmoons, moonitos, submoons, grandmoons, moonettes,* and *moooons.*

Saturn has the most moons. In 2019, this planet smashed Jupiter's record of seventy-nine moons when scientists discovered twenty new outer moons at Saturn. Added to Saturn's sixty-two previously known moons, the grand total equals eighty-two moons!

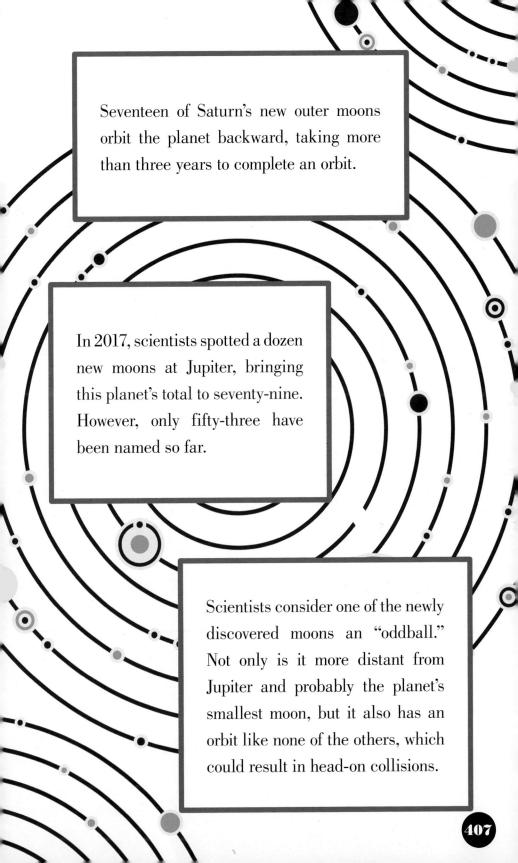

Seventeen of Saturn's new outer moons orbit the planet backward, taking more than three years to complete an orbit.

In 2017, scientists spotted a dozen new moons at Jupiter, bringing this planet's total to seventy-nine. However, only fifty-three have been named so far.

Scientists consider one of the newly discovered moons an "oddball." Not only is it more distant from Jupiter and probably the planet's smallest moon, but it also has an orbit like none of the others, which could result in head-on collisions.

Jupiter's four biggest moons are collectively called the Galilean satellites in honor of the astronomer who first observed them. These moons, in order of increasing distance from Jupiter, are Io, Europa, Ganymede, and Callisto.

Ganymede is the largest known moon in the solar system. This Galilean moon is even bigger than the planet Mercury!

The second largest moon—Titan—orbits Saturn. This moon has rivers, seas, and lakes—the only place besides Earth that has liquids on its surface!

Mercury and Venus, the two planets closest to the sun, lack moons. Since Mercury is closest to the sun and its gravity, any moon would either crash into the planet or be captured by the sun. Scientists believe that Venus once had a moon that formed the same way Earth's moon did, but Venus's moon collided and merged with the planet.

Pluto was once considered the ninth planet, but in 2006 it was stripped of its planetary status and renamed a dwarf planet.

Pluto is tiny—about 1,400 miles wide. That's only about half the width of the United States.

Time moves slowly on Pluto, compared to Earth. You'd have to live the equivalent of 248 Earth years on Pluto to celebrate your first birthday!

NASA's *New Horizons* spacecraft took a journey to Pluto that was more than three billion miles long, blasting off from Cape Canaveral, Florida, in 2006. That trip took nearly ten years.

If you wanted to fly to Pluto aboard a plane traveling at a maximum velocity of 590 miles per hour, it would take you a tad longer: 680 years!

New Horizons sent images of Pluto back to Earth. One showed a huge white "heart" more than one thousand miles wide. This was actually a heart-shaped glacier—the biggest in our solar system. The ice on Pluto is made of nitrogen, not water.

An eleven-year-old British girl gave Pluto its name in 1930. Venetia Burney suggested that the new discovery be named for the Roman god of the underworld.

The number of known planets in our galaxy rose to more than 1,700 in 2014. That's when astronomers discovered 715 new planets outside of Earth's solar system.

At least four of the new planets exist in the "Goldilocks zone," a region of space that can support life. Like in the fairy tale, these planets have to have the right qualities: neither too hot nor too cold, neither too large nor too small. Planets in this zone need the right temperatures for water to remain liquid.

The eight planets in our solar system share a few characteristics such as orbiting around a star—our sun—but each is unique. Let's explore them, from closest to farthest from the sun.

1. Mercury is not only the closest to the sun, but it's also the smallest planet in our solar system. It's only a tad larger than Earth's moon.
2. Mercury is the speediest of the planets, orbiting around the sun in only eighty-eight Earth days. This planet is named for the speedy Roman messenger god, who's portrayed wearing a winged cap and sandals.

3. The rocky surface of Mercury is covered in craters like our moon. Ice could be located deep inside craters that don't receive sunlight at this planet's north and south poles.

4. Mercury has the most extreme temperature swings of all the planets. Its surface can reach a broiling 800°F during the day and then plunge down to -290°F at night.

5. Even though Mercury is in closest proximity to the sun, it's not the hottest planet. That honor goes to Venus, the second closest to the sun.

6. The temperature on Venus is hot enough to melt lead into a liquid. Its surface sizzles with intense heat—around 900°F day and night.

7. Venus is the brightest planet in the sky and the third brightest object after the sun and moon.

8. This planet is the only one in our solar system to be named after a mythological goddess: Venus, the Roman goddess of love and beauty.

9. Venus spins in the opposite direction of most planets. That means that on this backward-rotating planet, the sun rises in the west and sets in the east.

10. Venus rotates slowly, taking 243 Earth days to spin around backward once. But it only takes 225 Earth days for Venus to orbit around the sun. That means that a day on Venus is longer than a year on Venus!

11. Our home planet, Earth, is the third from the sun—our local star. It's the only known planet to support life.

12. A famous photo of the Earth rising over the lunar landscape was taken from *Apollo 8,* the first manned mission to the moon, in December 1968. Titled *Earthrise,* it's the first full-color photo of our planet from more than 230,000 miles away.

13. When space rocks called meteoroids enter Earth's atmosphere, most burn up. Then we see "shooting stars"—the glowing hot air as the space rocks whizz through our atmosphere.

14. Unlike other planets, our home planet wasn't named after a Greek or Roman god or goddess. We don't know who named Earth, but its name is derived from Old English and German words that mean *ground.*

15. Earth's inner core is solid iron and nickel. These metals are as hot as the sun's surface, around 10,000°F.

16. The fourth planet from the sun is nicknamed the Red Planet. That's because the soil on Mars is a reddish color thanks to iron minerals that turn rusty. Mars was named after the Roman god of war because its color resembled blood.

17. Mars has a gigantic volcano, Olympus Mons, that's the largest in our solar system. It rises sixteen miles high—triple the height of Mount Everest (from sea level to summit).

18. The Martian surface is also home to the largest canyon. Valles Marineris stretches three thousand miles, about the distance from New York to California.

19. The gravity on Mars is much weaker than on Earth. You could jump three times higher on the Red Planet than on our home planet!

20. NASA sent its largest, most-advanced rover to the Red Planet. *Perseverance* touched down in 2021 after a 293-million-mile journey. This robotic geologist will hopefully pave the way for human missions.

21. Jupiter, the fifth planet from the sun, is also the largest and most massive. If you put all the other seven planets together, Jupiter would outweigh them by 2.5 times! No wonder this planet was named after the Roman king of the gods.

22. Although Jupiter is the king of planets size-wise, it has the shortest day of any other planet. It takes nine hours and fifty-five minutes for a complete rotation.

23. Jupiter's claim to fame is its Great Red Spot—a giant storm about twice the size of Earth that swirls around like a hurricane. This storm has been raging for more than three hundred years.

24. Jupiter also contains the largest ocean of any planet, but it's filled with liquid hydrogen instead of water.

25. Three different cloud layers make up Jupiter's skies. The top layer is the white cloud zone, made of ammonia ice.

26. The sixth planet from the sun, Saturn, is the most distant planet visible to the naked eye even though it's nearly a billion miles away! This planet was named after the Roman god of agriculture.

27. Saturn is nicknamed the Ringed Planet. It has spectacular rings made of chunks of ice and rocks that range in size from dust grains to bus-size particles.

28. Saturn's rings are enormous—about 240,000 miles wide, which is the distance from Earth to the moon! Yet the rings are extremely thin—their thickness is no more than 330 feet.

29. This giant gas planet is the only one in our solar system whose density is less than water's. If there was a bathtub big enough, Saturn could float in it!

30. NASA's Hubble Space Telescope captured an image of a ringless Saturn. This optical illusion happens twice every 29.5 years when the rings are tilted edge on.

31. William Herschel discovered Uranus, the seventh planet from the sun, in 1781. It was the first planet found using the aid of a telescope.

32. Several names were proposed for the planet, including Herschel and Georgium Sidus after King George III. Finally the scientific community accepted Uranus— the Greek god of the sky.

33. Uranus is nicknamed the Sideways Planet because it has a bizarre 98° tilt to its axis. A catastrophic collision with an ice planet might have caused Uranus to tip over and spin on its side.

34. Thanks to its sideways rotation, for half of its eighty-four-year orbit, the planet is constantly in the dark. For the next forty-two years, Uranus receives constant sunlight.

35. Uranus appears blue due to methane gas in its atmosphere. The methane absorbs the red light from the sun and reflects the blue light.

36. Neptune was named after the Roman god of the sea. Although the planet is the eighth and most distant from the sun, it's not the coldest planet. That honor goes to its neighbor Uranus.

37. Neptune is more than thirty times as far from the sun as Earth is. Our sunlight is more than nine hundred times brighter than Neptune's.

38. Supersonic winds whip Neptune at speeds of more than twelve hundred miles per hour. That's about five times stronger than Earth's most powerful winds.

39. One full orbit around the sun takes Neptune about 165 Earth years.

40. Some scientists believe that extreme temperature and pressure inside Neptune's core might cause diamonds to fall like raindrops toward the center of the planet.

A 1967 international law prevents any nation from owning planets, stars, moons, or any other natural objects in space.

You cannot measure the temperature of outer space—it's a vacuum with no matter. Only objects within space's vacuum have a temperature.

We have better maps of the surface of Mars and the moon than we do of the ocean floor, which we have only been able to map around 5 percent of.

Scientists estimate there are five to ten times more stars in space than grains of sand on Earth!

We are only able to see about 5 percent of the known universe. The remaining 95 percent is made up of dark matter and dark energy. They're both invisible even with powerful telescopes, but we know this dark sector is there.

You now know 81 facts about PECULIAR PLANETS AND MYSTERIOUS MOONS!

Stranger than Fiction

We wrap up with outrageous facts that sound unbelievable, proving that not only is truth stranger than fiction, but it's also far more remarkable than invented tales!

—

In 1945, a chicken farmer and his wife beheaded chickens, but one refused to die. The decapitated rooster got up and walked around! Miracle Mike the Headless Chicken went on a sideshow circuit touring the United States and went on to live an amazing eighteen months sans his head.

A person who suffers from boanthropy believes that he or she is a bovine: a cow, bull, or ox. This rare disorder causes the sufferer to walk on all fours, eat grass, join herds in the pasture, and start mooing.

Pastel-colored toilet paper first appeared in the 1950s when Americans color-coordinated their bathrooms. The trend ended in the 1980s because the colored dyes were harmful to people's skin and the environment.

While rolls of white toilet paper appear in American bathrooms, in France, pink is the regional preference for toilet paper. No one knows who started the trend for this color "bum paper."

America's first roller coaster was used to transport coal down the mountains of Pennsylvania in 1872. People clamored for rides aboard the Mauch Chunk Switchback Railway as it zoomed down a long inclined slope.

An eerie fourteenth-century bell tower rises out of Lake Resia in Italy, hinting at the drowned village below. Curon was flooded in 1950 to create a hydroelectric plant. The village briefly resurfaced after seventy years underwater, when the lake was drained for reservoir repairs.

A determined bridge engineer wanted to impress the world at the 1893 Chicago World's Fair with an invention that would rival the Eiffel Tower, the superstar of the last world's fair in Paris. George Ferris built his mechanical marvel with a new metal, steel, and his Ferris wheel continues to be a star attraction.

George Nissen invented a bouncing apparatus in his parents' garage when he was sixteen. He patented his trampoline in 1945, and his tumbling device became an Olympic sport in 2000.

The US military used trampolines as a training device for fighter pilots during World War II. Thanks to trampolines, pilots could practice pirouetting in midair to simulate difficult air maneuvers.

Later, NASA introduced trampolines for space-training future astronauts. Nissen and a pilot friend invented a fun game called Spaceball using a three-sided trampoline as a conditioning exercise for space travel.

Astronauts in training rode aboard modified ex-military aircraft that pilots flew in a wavelike motion to simulate near-weightlessness for twenty to twenty-five seconds. This experience caused about one in three first-time fliers to become airsick, earning the plane the nickname Vomit Comet.

A female Fernandina giant tortoise astonished scientists on an expedition to the Galápagos Islands. They had believed that this species went extinct in 1906.

The world's longest human chain stretched 652.4 miles across Bangladesh, with more than five million people joining hands.

Two huge rocks in Saudi Arabia precariously balance on natural pedestals and are split apart by a thin, perfectly vertical gap. The Al Naslaa Rock Formation took centuries to acquire its shape and features a petroglyph of a horse on its surface.

Although Manhattan island is 1 percent of the size of Yellowstone National Park, it once had fifty-five ecosystems. Yellowstone has sixty-six within its 2.2 million acres.

If bees earned a minimum wage for their labor, one jar of honey would cost $182,000.

Albino animals lack melanin in their skin, but some animals produce too much of this skin pigment. This condition is called melanism. Animals evolved to sport dark skin, hair, fur, and feathers so they're better camouflaged.

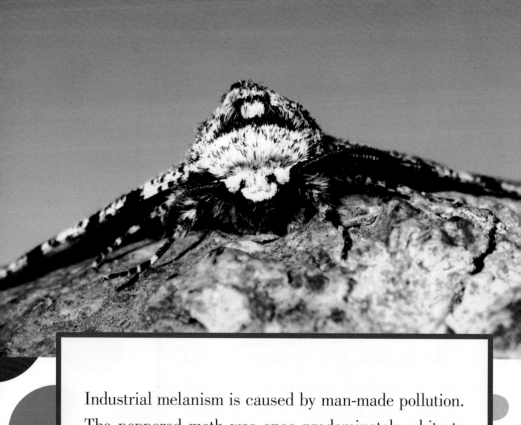

Industrial melanism is caused by man-made pollution. The peppered moth was once predominately white to blend in with lichen covered trees in England. But when coal soot started covering the trees and killing the lichens, darker moths were less visible to predators. Soon the black peppered moths outnumbered white ninety-nine to one.

An unbelievable 7 percent of American adults think that chocolate milk comes from brown cows! That works out to 16.4 million people who lack an understanding of basic science.

The snakes in China can predict earthquakes up to five days before they occur! According to scientists, the serpents start behaving erratically—smashing into walls on snake farms and moving out of nests even in winter.

How does the Tennessee Aquarium ID their American alligators at a glance? During physical exams, staff gives each gator a set of different-colored nail caps!

There were real fortunes in cookies made in New York. In 2005, 110 Powerball players who used the lucky numbers printed on the slips of paper inside their fortune cookies claimed prizes of either $110,000 or $500,000. The fortune cookies foretold five out of the six lottery numbers.

Scientists discovered the secret behind why flamingos balance on one long spindly leg while sleeping. It turns out that this position is easier for the big birds to balance their bodies than standing on two legs.

One species of jellyfish is immortal. This sea animal can revert back to its immature stage even after becoming an adult.

If you've stayed up nights puzzling why doughnuts have holes, there's a simple explanation: uneven cooking. The center of the donut dough cooks slower than the perimeter so the donut hole was born.

Or maybe you've wondered why bananas are curved. The answer is also easy peasy: when the fruits grow in size, they turn toward the sun to receive sunlight through the rainforest canopy.

Who's the first nonhuman mammal to keep the beat? That would be Ronan the California sea lion, who can out-head-bob the most rhythmic human to the beat of "Boogie Wonderland"!

A stray sheep living in the Australian wild was rescued and liberated from seventy-eight pounds of wool! Baarack can finally see again after his shearing.

The original London Bridge really was falling down, so an American oil tycoon purchased the ten-thousand-ton bridge and had it shipped to and reassembled in an Arizona desert town. The cost? Some $7 million!

More than half of all Icelanders believe in the existence of elves. Stories of elves and other "hidden people" date back to around 1,000 CE in the Nordic island country.

A smart eleven-year-old girl came up with the Pinocchio paradox, a seemingly absurd or contradictory statement that actually proves to be true. The wooden puppet's nose grows when he tells a lie. He can only cause a paradox by saying, "My nose will grow now." Pinocchio's nose would have to grow to make his statement *true*. However, the only way his nose will grow is if he lies; that's why it's a paradox.

A crane operates the world's largest working yo-yo. This gargantuan toy weighs 4,620 pounds— about the weight of an adult rhino!

The island of Saint Lucia in the Caribbean is the only country in the world named after a woman.

Scripps Institution of Oceanography at University of California, San Diego, has an underwater library containing approximately two million alcohol-preserved fish in 140,000 jars. The specimens, representing more than six thousand different marine fish species, are all available to the scientific community.

Super-size pumpkins can gain up to sixty pounds a day during peak growing cycle.

The shortest two words in English are the article *a* and the pronoun I.

The longest word in English would span about fifty-seven pages! This word—a chemical name for a giant elastic protein—has 189,819 letters in its full name. A man sounds it out on a YouTube video that lasts 3 hours, 33 minutes, and 22 seconds.

The tallest snowman rose up 124.8 feet in an Austrian ski region. Nicknamed Riesi, or *giant* in English, the colossal snowman was created by builders using snow cannons.

Squirrels are responsible for 10 percent to 20 percent of all power outages. The rodents never stop teething on those tasty wires.

Honeybees can recognize and remember different human faces through shape and pattern.

Eating too many carrots can turn your skin a cartoonish orange! But you'd have to consume around ten of these beta-carotene-rich veggies per day for a few weeks to turn this hue.

Pirates wore earrings because they believed that the precious metals would magically cure bad eyesight, aid in seasickness, and prevent drowning.

Adam Rainer is the only human recorded to have both dwarfism and gigantism. At the age of 18 he measured 4 feet ¼ inches, but a genetic condition later resulted in a remarkable growth spurt, and Adam measured 7 feet 8 inches!

Thousands of people embarked on a treasure hunt in the Rocky Mountains after Forrest Fenn hid a chest filled with more than $1 million worth of gold and precious gems. He published cryptic clues about its location in his autobiography. After a ten-year search, a lucky treasure hunter located the precise spot where the chest had been hidden.

What in the world is paraskevidekatriaphobia? This unpronounceable phobia is fear of Friday the Thirteenth and it apparently affects millions of Americans.

Typewriter is the longest word you can type using one row of letters.

Americans eat one hundred acres of pizza every day—that's forty-six slices for every person in the country annually!

The oldest known animal in the world hatched before the light bulb was invented! Jonathan, a Seychelles giant tortoise, was born in 1832 and spends his days relaxing with his reptile buddies on the remote island of Saint Helena.

An eleven-year-old boy accidentally invented the Popsicle back in 1905. He mixed sugary soda powder with water and left the cup with its wooden stirrer outside one freezing night. The next morning—eureka—the Popsicle was born!

Today it's "cheese," but back in the Victorian era photographers asked their subjects to say "prunes." Then, instead of flashing smiles, people kept their mouths taut. Smiles weren't in vogue back then and besides, most Victorians had dental decay.

The Statue of Liberty in New York Harbor served as a working lighthouse from 1886 to 1902. But Lady Liberty made a terrible lighthouse—her beacon was too weak to act as a navigational aid.

Shell Oil Company built eight gas stations shaped like huge yellow scallop shells as a marketing gimmick to lure in customers back in the 1930s. The last remaining station still stands in Winston-Salem, North Carolina, but it no longer sells gas.

Not only was Frances Glessner Lee the first female US police captain, but she was also the "mother of forensic science." The detailed dollhouse-size crime scenes that she crafted in the 1940s and 1950s continue to be used to teach investigators how to uncover evidence in unexplained deaths.

What's the one letter of the alphabet that doesn't appear in any US state names? If you guessed *Q* you're correct.

A few rare puppies enter this world with green fur! A green bile pigment in the mother's placenta causes the unusual hue, which soon fades.

Pizza Hut became the first restaurant chain to deliver to outer space, when it sent a pie to the International Space Station in 2001. The pizza took a tad longer than the usual thirty-minute delivery time and arrived via a rocket used to resupply the station.

A flawed gene causes one breed of domestic rabbits to hop on their front paws with their back legs held high in a handstand pose. Scientists are studying this mutation to learn more about how the spinal cord works.

The world's first underwater post office operated on the seafloor of the Bahamas in 1939.

Pogonophobia is the fear of beards. Perhaps the phobic person felt anxious after learning that beards contain more harmful bacteria than dog fur.

Most pigeons are garbed in brown, gray, black, and white feathers. Not the pink-necked green pigeon, who's found in Southeast Asia. These stunning birds sport plumage in rainbow shades of blue, green, lilac, pink, and yellow.

Archaeologists discovered the world's oldest perfumes inside the ruins of an ancient Cyprus factory destroyed in an earthquake. Perfumers re-created some of these four-thousand-year-old aromas that were made with herbal extracts.

Severe weather caused a shipping crate filled with twenty-nine thousand plastic yellow ducks, green frogs, red beavers, and blue turtles to fall from a cargo ship in 1992. For decades later, the bath toys floated and, carried by global ocean currents, washed up on coastlines across half the world.

Sailors call shipping containers bobbing on the ocean "steel icebergs." An average of 1,382 containers are lost per year, causing environmental hazards. According to one oceanographer, each spill is equivalent to dumping an entire big box store into the ocean.

Time passes faster on top of a mountain than down below on a beach. That's because the gravity of a large mass, like Earth, has the power to warp time and space—just as Einstein posited in his theory of general relativity.

A woman in South Africa smashed a world record in 2021 when she gave birth to ten babies at once. The decuplets are thought to be the first in history.

Sheepshead fish have bizarre chompers: their giant molar-like teeth make them look as if they've swallowed dentures! Plus their powerful jaws allow them to snap metal fish hooks in half.

Archaeologists in England discovered a sharpened crayon used by Mesolithic humans ten thousand years ago. The ancient crayon had a reddish-brown pigment made from clay and sand.

In the deep ocean a tsunami can travel at speeds of more than five hundred miles per hour—as fast as a jet plane.

According to the Food and Drug Administration's "Defect Levels Handbook," low levels of icky stuff are allowed to be present in your food. For example, 100 grams of peanut butter can contain thirty or more insect fragments and one or more rodent hairs. Yuck!

You could wash down that peanut butter sandwich with the world's most expensive tea. The special blend of green tea is fertilized using panda poop and costs around $35,000 per pound!

You already know that platypuses are odd-ball mammals, but they got even stranger when researchers discovered that their fur glows blue and green under ultraviolet light.

Lunar rainbows are called moonbows. They form in the same way as the familiar rainbows we see after daytime thunderstorms, but the light comes from the moon instead of the sun. Since there is less light at night, the colors in moonbows are less vibrant.

It sounds like the punch line to a joke, but it could be a *Jeopardy* clue: a sheep, a duck, and a rooster. The correct response: What are the first hot-air balloon passengers?

Although European starlings are regarded as invasive pests, they're amazingly skilled in mimicry. These birds imitate human voices, dog barks, frog ribbits, car horns, and more!

A tree could explode if lightning strikes deep into its trunk. First the water inside the tree cells boils and turns into steam, which causes a spike in pressure, and then *kaboom!*

Some 4 percent to 14 percent of people inherited a gene that makes the herb cilantro taste like soap.

Nine out of the ten most common birthdays in the world occur in the month of September.

Two students pranked curators at an art gallery when they left a pineapple on an empty stand. The staff mistook the fruit for modern art and placed it under glass, making "Pineapple on a Pedestal" part of the gallery exhibit.

Around 2 percent of people are "super recognizers"—they have an uncanny ability to recognize faces of people they've only briefly encountered and haven't seen for decades. This superpower could help catch criminals by scanning crowds for wanted perpetrators.

Another 2 percent of the population has "face blindness"—an inability to remember faces, sometimes not even recognizing family members.

The North American curly horse looks like a cousin to the labradoodle. This affectionate breed once roamed wild in the Northern Plains. The horse has a curly coat, including inside the ears, and is hypoallergenic.

A photo called *Stars and Stripes Sunset* was snapped in Oklahoma on the eve of the tenth anniversary of September 11. The sky resembled an American flag thanks to clouds forming red and white stripes against a deep blue background.

If you need a laparoscopy—a surgical procedure using a mini video camera that sends images to a computer screen—make sure the surgeon plays video games! The hand-eye coordination skills are similar for performing surgery and playing video games. Surgeons who play video games at least three hours per week make 37 percent fewer mistakes and perform the surgery 27 percent faster than those who don't play.

You now know 83 facts that are STRANGER THAN FICTION!

Index

—